Religion in Human Culture

The Islamic Tradition

WORLD RELIGIONS CURRICULUM DEVELOPMENT CENTER
MINNEAPOLIS, MINNESOTA

Project Co-Directors: Lee Smith and Wes Bodin
Project Assistants: Joan Voigt and Pat Noyes

Argus Communications
Allen, Texas 75002 U.S.A.

Photo Credits

Cover Photos

H. Follo/BLACK STAR   middle
C. Henneghien/BRUCE COLEMAN INC.   lower right
John Launois/BLACK STAR   bottom
Jean-Claude LeJeune   top, lower left

Page Photos

6 Phedon Salou/SHOSTAL ASSOCIATES
11 Ernest Manewal/SHOSTAL ASSOCIATES
12 THE BETTMANN ARCHIVE
15 John J. Cumming
19 H. D. Shourie/SHOSTAL ASSOCIATES
23 Arabian-American Oil Company
   (ARAMCO)
30 MEDIA RESOURCES CATALOGUE
31 Trustees of the British Museum, London
34 C. A. Kennedy/MEDIA
   RESOURCES CATALOGUE
38 Bernard Pierre Wolff/ALPHA
   PHOTO ASSOCIATES, INC.
40 L. A. Mayer Memorial Institute for
   Islamic Art

43 Ray Manley/SHOSTAL ASSOCIATES
47 John J. Cumming
50 Charles Harbutt/MAGNUM PHOTOS
54 A. Florey/BRUCE COLEMAN INC.
62 SHOSTAL ASSOCIATES
67 Bruce L. Beregan/SHOSTAL ASSOCIATES
71 SHOSTAL ASSOCIATES
75 SHEIKH PUBLICATIONS
78 C. Mouhd/DIWAN PRESS
79/82 SHEIKH PUBLICATIONS
84 D. Von Knobloch/SHOSTAL ASSOCIATES
86 K. Scholz/SHOSTAL ASSOCIATES
91 Mickey Mathis/SHOSTAL ASSOCIATES
95 Robert D. Baird
98 P. Schmid/SHOSTAL ASSOCIATES
103 Richard W. Wilkie/BLACK STAR
107 David Warren/SHOSTAL ASSOCIATES
110 SHOSTAL ASSOCIATES
115 H. D. Shourie/SHOSTAL ASSOCIATES
118/122 K. Scholz/SHOSTAL ASSOCIATES
126 SHOSTAL ASSOCIATES

Acknowledgments

Excerpts from *Islam in Focus* by Hammudah Abdalati. Copyright © 1975 by American Trust Publications. Reprinted by permission of The Muslim Students' Association of the United States and Canada, Plainfield, Indiana.

Excerpts from Islamic Correspondence Course. Copyright © 1974 by the Muslim Students' Association of the United States and Canada, Plainfield, Indiana. Reprinted by permission.

Excerpt from *The Conception of God in Islam* by Dr. Ali Abdel Kader. Adapted and reprinted by permission of The Islamic Center, Washington, D.C.

Excerpts from *A Short History of Islam* by Sayyid Fayyaz Mahmud. Copyright © 1960 by Oxford University Press. Reprinted by permission of Oxford University Press, Pakistan.

Excerpt from *Towards Understanding Islam*, 9th ed., by Abul A'la Maududi, trans. and ed. by Khurshid Ahmad. Copyright by Islamic Publications Limited. Reprinted by permission of The Islamic Foundation, Leicester, U.K.

Calendar of Ramadan 1397 (1977). Reprinted by permission of The Islamic Center, Washington, D.C.

Excerpts from *Islam Creed and Worship* by Muhammad Abdul Rauf. Copyright © 1974 by Muhammad Abdul Rauf. Reprinted by permission of The Islamic Center, Washington, D.C.

Excerpts from "This Is Islam" by Zeba Siddiqui (to be published by the Muslim Students' Association of the United States and Canada). Adapted and used by permission of the author.

Religion in Human Culture is a project of St. Louis Park Independent School District #283, Title III/IV (Part C), ESEA, and the Northwest Area Foundation. The opinions and other contents of this book do not necessarily reflect the position or policy of the State of Minnesota, the U.S. Government, St. Louis Park ISD #283, or the Northwest Area Foundation, and no official endorsement should be inferred.

Design by Gene Tarpey
Map by Homer Grooman

Argus Communications
One DLM Park
Allen, Texas 75002

International Standard Book Number:
0-89505-009-9

Library of Congress Number:
78-50915

0 9 8 7 6 5 4 3 2

Contents

Note to the Reader

The general purpose of this book is to acquaint you with many of the general characteristics of Islam. It seems impossible to find out all there is to know about Islam in a relatively short book. The hope is that those who read this book will raise questions, become interested in finding answers, and personally seek out more information. Since this book focuses on the general characteristics of Islam, the diversity within this tradition is not treated.

This book contains material written by Muslims about their own beliefs, and the reader needs to keep that fact in mind. These authors are very involved in Islam and are attempting to tell other Muslims, as well as non-Muslims, what is necessary to be a true follower of Islam. Some of the readings are written specifically for Muslims, and the non-Muslim needs to take that into consideration. The purpose of these readings is to present an accurate account of Islam and of Muslim attitudes toward Islam and thereby to increase understanding between the Muslim and non-Muslim.

A few other clarifications about the readings should be made. First, the spelling of some words may vary from one reading to another or from these readings to other sources on Islam—for example, Muhammad-Mohammed, Ka'aba-Ka'bah, and Qur'an-Koran. Such variations in spelling results from transliterating Arabic words into English. Keep in mind that these are the same words and only the spelling is different. Also, all references to God or Allah are capitalized in the readings, following the traditional Muslim style. Finally, the customary diacritical marks have not been used in this book, but you have probably seen, or will see, these marks in other materials on Islam. The purpose of the diacritical marks is to show pronunciation and the accented syllable—for example, Islām, Qur'ān, Allāh.

Remember that this book comes from a variety of authors and consists of a series of readings. Therefore, it cannot be read like a textbook or novel. To facilitate your reading, a glossary of many terms relevant to Islam is provided at the back of this book.

READING 1
The Islamic Creed*
ZEBA SIDDIQUI

The Islamic creed or declaration of faith is generally considered to be the first of the Pillars of Islam. Although the Pillars of Islam are the focus of Part II of this book, the creed is introduced here because it is so central to the Islamic tradition.

La ilaha illa Allah, Muhammadur Rasul Allah. ("There is no deity except God, Muhammad is the Messenger of God.")

This simple statement of the basic beliefs of Islam is the starting point for all that follows. From this expression of belief in the Oneness of God and the prophethood of Muhammad stem all Islamic concepts, attitudes, values, behavior, and relationships.

How can all this follow from this one simple statement? Thus. To a Muslim the conviction of the Oneness of God also signifies the oneness of the lordship and sovereignty over the universe and humankind. For God is not only the Creator and Sustainer of the universe, this world, and everything in it; He is also the Lawgiver, the sole and supreme Authority and Ruler of all humankind. Human beings are created to worship and serve Him, and they occupy the position of God's servants, placed on earth to govern it according to His laws with decency and justice. And as God is

*From Zeba Siddiqui, "This Is Islam" (to be published by the Muslim Students' Association of the United States and Canada).

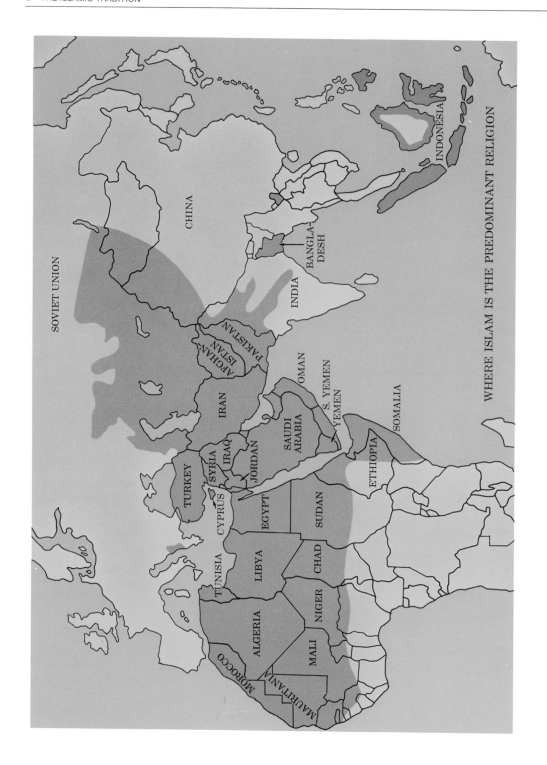

WHERE ISLAM IS THE PREDOMINANT RELIGION

One, so also is humanity, His creation, one—all people living together on this planet under His providence.

How does one know all this? How can a limited and finite human being, whose body and mental faculties can extend but a very little distance into the vast complexity of all that exists, know about God—that is, about Infinity? These are important questions, certainly, ones which every thinking person must ask and seek to answer.

Islam emphasizes that there is no way by which we can know any or all of this by our own searching, deduction, or faculties. The only way we can know about it is if the Source of everything, God Himself, reveals it to us. And this is the significance of the second part of the Muslim's declaration of faith—*Muhammadur Rasul Allah* ("Muhammad is the Messenger of God").

Since the very beginning of human history, Islam teaches, God chose men from among humankind to bring His message to various peoples. Much of this message was lost over a period of time, due to inaccurate transmission or deliberate or accidental changes. However, enough remains of the scriptures or teachings of the early prophets—such as Abraham, Moses, and Jesus—to make it very clear that this message has always been one and the same throughout history: that of the Oneness of God and the duty of all human beings to obey Him and follow His guidance. *Islam,* then, which in Arabic means "submission," "acceptance," and "peace," is the name given to this message. Those who profess Islam—that is, those who submit to the One True God—are called Muslims (not Mohammedans).

Thus it can be seen that Islam does not claim to be a new religion. Rather, the Qur'an repeatedly asserts that it is the same religion revealed by God to all the prophets, namely, the religion of submission to God. Islam teaches the Divine origin of this message, pointing to the similarity and continuity of the teachings brought by the various prophets. But it states that in the course of time these teachings were changed and distorted. Thus their Divine origin is to be believed in, but not necessarily their present form or content, since it is not clear what part has been changed.

According to Islam, each of the prophets was a man having the same human needs and feelings as other men. The concept of prophethood in Islam is utterly opposed to any suggestion of the divinity or superhuman nature of God's messengers. Yet the prophets were very special human beings, since God singled them out from the rest of humankind for the task of conveying His guidance. They were also unique because of their absolute righteousness and the devotion with which they carried out their missions.

Finally, when humanity had developed to the point where it could fully grasp the reality of a noncorporeal, transcendent God, and could accept the responsibility of total submission to Him, God chose to send His last prophet, Muhammad, with the final revelation. And it is because Muslims follow the guidance which came through Muhammad, the guidance which conveys the final statement of God's purposes, laws, and commands for human-kind, that *Muhammadur Rasul Allah* is so significant and vital as to form the second part of the Muslim's declaration of faith.

La ilaha illa Allah, Muhammadur Rasul Allah, then, is to the Muslim the denial of all other claimants to divinity and supreme authority except the One God, and the affirmation of God's absolute Oneness and Sovereignty. It is also the statement of belief in, and acceptance of, His guidance as revealed to Prophet Muhammad, the last of His messengers.

PART I

The Articles of Faith in Islam

There are specific basic beliefs in Islam that Muslims feel are extremely important, and these beliefs are referred to as the Articles of Faith. Muslims believe that Muhammad asked them to believe in these Articles of Faith and that the true, faithful Muslim does believe in them. Most of the authors who have written explanations of these Articles of Faith concentrate on either five or six articles. Part I of this book presents six: (1) the Oneness of God, (2) the revealed books, (3) the prophets, (4) the angels, (5) the hereafter, and (6) Qadar, or God's decrees. Note that there is no set sequence that the Articles of Faith must follow, which accounts for the differing order found in various explanations.

A pattern of arches distinguishes this mosque in Marrakesh, Morocco.

READING 2
The Conception of God in Islam*
DR. ALI ABDEL KADER

The conception of God in Islam is based on the belief that there is an *unseen* order. This religious attitude can be analysed into three points: *first,* the reality of the *unseen* behind and above our ordinary experience, which is the background to life, and which is unattainable to our physical senses; *second,* man's relation to the *unseen*—his faith and insight; . . . and *lastly,* the discipline of the worshipper on his way to attain a direct knowledge of God during his life.

But before dealing with these points, the differences should be made clear in the conception of the *unseen* in the Eastern and modern Western thought and experience. To the Oriental mind, the supernatural is the familiar, the usual. It is not subject to reason, and the Oriental never dreams that it could be. The attitude to the *unseen* held by Eastern and Western people is different intellectually, socially, and from a religious point of view. When the Oriental is confronted by things which he cannot explain, he accepts them as such, believing that they spring directly from the will of God. The Western mind, on the other hand, feels vaguely that there is a divine element in the world, but it is far off. An impenetrable shell separates him from that fact. To the Muslim, this shell does not exist, as he believes that all his actions and reactions spring from the immediate will of God. . . .

*Adapted from Dr. Ali Abdel Kader, *The Conception of God in Islam* (Washington, D.C.: The Islamic Center, n.d.), pp. 8–12.

Now what is this conception of God in Islam? According to Islam, God alone exists absolutely. Everything else that we may find to exist does so only through His will. In other words, He has created all other things, or may create them in the future. The very essence of God is *existence,* and all created things have only an existence derived from him. Judaism, Christianity and Islam accept this. So does Hinduism, Zarathustra, Greek philosophy and the teachers of China.

To have knowledge of the works of God and of his powers is not yet the same as to have a knowledge and awareness of the being or essence of God. Yet the lack of our complete knowledge of God does not destroy the value of that knowledge as far as it goes. It is plain in Islam that God exists, but what He is in essence and nature is not completely comprehensible.

The Qur'an stresses the *Oneness* of God and it is this which characterises the preaching of the Prophet Muhammad. He is One; He is *the One* (Qur'an 40:16 and 112:1); He cannot be imagined as having any peer or equal or similar.

God says in the Qur'an: "Say, 'Praise be due to God, and peace be upon His servants whom He has chosen.' Is God better or what they associate with Him? He who created the Heavens and the Earth and sends down on you rain from Heaven whereby We cause to grow gardens fraught with beauty; ye could not cause the trees thereof to grow. Is there a god with God? Nay, but they are a people who make peers with him. He who made the earth firm to live in; made rivers in its midst; set therein firm mountains, and placed between the two seas a barrier, is there a god with God? Nay, but most of them know not. He who answers the prayers of the distressed when he calls upon Him and removes the suffering and makes you successors in the earth, is there a god with God?" (Sura xxii, 59–62.); "God, there is no god but He, the Living, the Self-subsistent. Slumber overtakes Him not, nor sleep. His is what is in the heavens and what is in the earth. Who is it that intercedes with Him, without His permission? He knows what is before them and what is behind them and they comprehend naught of His knowledge but of what He pleases. His throne extends over the heavens and the earth, and it tires Him not to guard them both, for He is High and Grand" (Sura ii, 255); "Do they associate with Him things which cannot create anything, but they themselves are created, and which have no power to help or themselves?" (Sura vii, 191). Besides these passages of the Qur'an there are many other passages proclaiming the *Oneness* of God. This is asserted against paganism and also against those who associate others with God, and against dualism. However, it is stated in many verses of the Qur'an that the God of the Jews and Christians is Allah, the One True God.

In Islam very great stress is laid on the *Oneness* of God—in worship, prayer, meditation, thought, religious service and everyday life. The Muslim faces the One God, he confides in Him, concentrates upon Him in his worship and continually seeks and appreciates Him in daily life. . . .

Regarding the Attributes of God, the Qur'an states that God is Almighty, He is Omni-present, He is Eternal. He is at the same time Transcendent and Immanent. He is yonder, and He is here, with us—at all times. He is Personality, yet should by no means be conceived as anthropomorphic [having human traits].

God is manifest. He reveals Himself continuously in Nature and in Creation. He also reveals Himself in Revelation, in the Revelations given by Him to the Prophets before Muhammad, and in the Holy Qur'an, the final Revelation which was given by God to Muhammad. . . .

To sum up, Muslims of all walks of life, simple people, thinkers, philosophers, have all clung to this primary belief and experience—the *Oneness* of God, which characterises the Creed of Islam. All Muslim schools of thought and social and political groups, all accept this and they are all held together within this idea—the Unity of God.

The Islamic Creed regarding the Conception of God, as described in the following passages by Al-Ghazzali, the leading Muslim thinker of the 11th Century A.D., can give us a very clear and subtle systematic form, universally accepted by every Muslim.

PART OF A SHORT CREED BY AL-GHAZZALI

God in His essence is One without any partner; Single without any similar, Eternal without any opposite, Separate without any like. He is One; prior with nothing before Him, from eternity; without any beginning, abiding in existence with none after Him; in Eternity, without any end, subsisting without ending, abiding without termination. He hath not ceased, and He will not cease to be described with glorious epithets. He is the First and the Last, the Evident and the Immanent and He knoweth everything.

We witness that He is not a body possessing form, nor a substance possessing bounds and limits: He does not resemble bodies either in limitation or in accepting division. He is not a substance and substances do not exist in Him. Nay, He does not resemble an entity, and no entity resembles Him; nothing is like Him and He is not like anything; measure does not limit Him and boundaries do not contain Him; the directions do not surround Him and neither the earth nor heavens are on different sides of Him.

There is not in His essence His equal, nor in His equal His essence. He is far removed from change of state or of place. Events have no place in Him and mishaps do not befall Him. Nay, He does not cease, through His glorious qualities, to be far removed from changing, and through His perfect qualities to be independent of perfecting increase.

We witness that He is living, powerful, commanding; inadequacy and weakness befall Him not; slumber seizes Him not, nor sleep. Passing away does not happen to Him, nor death. He is the Lord of the Worlds, the visible world and the invisible, that of force and that of might; He possesses rule, creation and command: He created the creatures and their works, and decreed their sustenance and their terms of life.

We witness that He knoweth all the things that can be known, comprehending that which happeneth from the bounds of the earth unto the highest heavens; no grain in the earth or the heavens is distant from His knowledge; yea, He knows the creeping of the little ant upon the rugged rock in a dark night, and He perceives the movement of the mote in the midst of the air; He knows the secret and the concealed and has knowledge of the suggestions of the minds and the movements of the thoughts and the concealed thing of the inmost parts, by a knowledge which is prior from eternity.

We witness that He is a Willer of the things that are, and of the things that happen; there does not come about in the world, seen or unseen, little or much, small or great, good or evil, advantage or disadvantage, faith or unbelief, knowledge or ignorance, success or loss, increase or diminution, obedience or rebellion, except by His will. What He wills is, and what He wills not is not. Not a glance of one who looks, or a slip of one who thinks is outside His will: He is the Creator, the Bringer back, the Doer of that which He wills.

And we witness that He is The All Hearing, The All Seeing, and no audible thing is distant from His hearing, and no visible thing is far from His seeing, however fine it may be. Distance does not curtain off His hearing, and darkness does not dull his seeing.

And we witness that He speaks, commanding, forbidding, praising, threatening, with a speech from all eternity, prior, subsisting in His essence, not resembling the speech of created things. He is Living, Knowing, Powerful, a Willer, a Hearer, a Seer, a Speaker through Life, Power, Knowledge, Will, Hearing, Seeing, Speech, not by a thing separated from His essence.

A Yugoslavian Muslim picks up his shoes after prayers. Muslims are instructed by the Prophet Muhammad to pray in bare or stockinged feet.

A page from a thirteenth-century Qur'an.

READING 3A

The Revealed Books*

ZEBA SIDDIQUI

Among many others, the following passage from the Holy Qur'an relates to the divinely revealed scriptures.

> It was We[1] Who revealed the law (to Moses). Therein was guidance and light. . . . And in their (the Prophets') footsteps We sent Jesus the son of Mary, confirming the law that had come before him (the revelation to Moses). We sent him the *Injil* (revelation given to Jesus); therein was guidance and an admonition to those who fear God. . . . To thee (Muhammad) We sent the scripture (the Qur'an) in truth, confirming the scripture that had come before it, and guarding it in safety. . . . (5:47, 49, 51)

We have already discussed the Islamic belief in the oneness and continuity of the Divine guidance throughout the history of humanity. For only God Himself—the only One Who knows everything and Who alone is able to determine what is beneficial and harmful for His creations, including human beings—could provide such guidance.

Islam teaches that God's guidance was transmitted to the prophets through the agency of the Angel Gabriel (*Jibril* in Arabic). The final guidance—the Holy Qur'an revealed to Prophet Muhammad—was also brought by the Angel Gabriel. The angel frequently appeared to the Prophet in his true angelic form or in

*From Zeba Siddiqui, "This Is Islam" (to be published by the Muslim Students' Association of the United States and Canada).
[1]God refers to Himself in the Holy Qur'an interchangeably as "We," "He," and "I."

the form of a man. While the revelations were being transmitted to him, Muhammad would often undergo noticeable physical changes which were at times observed and documented by many of his companions.

Qur'an (often Anglicized and spelled and pronounced "Koran") is an Arabic word meaning "that which is to be read." The Qur'an was revealed to Prophet Muhammad over a period of twenty-three years between 609 and 632 After Christ. It came to him in parts bearing an intimate relationship to the events that the Prophet and his community, the first Muslims, were encountering at the time. Although many portions are closely tied to the context in which they were revealed, all rules and prohibitions are binding on Muslims of all times and places.

The Qur'an speaks of the attributes of God, and of His power and creativity. It discusses the relationship and responsibility of human beings to Him, and the certainty of the coming of the Day of Judgment when all people will stand before God to receive their reward or punishment according to their intentions and actions in this life. The Qur'an guides all aspects of human relationships and provides the moral principles to govern human behavior, both individual and collective. It also narrates the histories of some of the earlier prophets as an example and encouragement to the Prophet and his community, as well as a warning to those who deny God.

Islam asserts that the Holy Qur'an is the only divinely revealed scripture that has been preserved in its exact original form throughout human history. That the Qur'an has retained the exact wording revealed to Prophet Muhammad, and the exact order in which he himself placed its parts as commanded by Divine revelation, is well documented. Concerning earlier revelations, Islam states that parts of such divinely revealed scriptures as the Torah *(Taurat)* given to Moses, the Psalms *(Zabur)* revealed to David, and the sayings of Jesus (known as the *Injil)* remain, although intermixed with human additions and changes.

Because the Qur'an is the speech of God, it is always recited in Arabic, the language in which it was revealed. It is quoted in the Muslim prayers *(Salat)* and on other occasions, but never in translation. It may, however, be read in translation for the understanding of those who do not know Arabic. But all Muslim scholars agree that because of its depth of meaning and

The first chapter of the Qur'an.

distinctive style and language, it is impossible for a translation to do more than convey its bare meanings. Its deep concepts and ideas, distinctive form of expression, and the eloquent, moving, earnest tone, which are its outstanding characteristics, cannot be translated. Hence any translation must be regarded (as all translators themselves admit only too freely) as a mere approximation to the sense of the words. While Islam does not rest its credibility on miracles or on signs and wonders, many who are familiar with Arabic literary style regard the Qur'an itself as a miracle—a work which cannot be attributed to human authorship, so unparalleled is its language and form of expression. When one looks at the sayings of Muhammad *(Hadith)* side-by-side with the Qur'an, there is simply no basis for comparison. The one is obviously the ordinary, everyday speech of a man, while the style of the Qur'an is so lofty and striking that it is impossible to suppose that a human being could have authored it.

The Holy Qur'an says:

It is He Who sent down to thee (Muhammad) the Book. In it are verses basic or fundamental; they are the foundation of the Book. Others are allegorical. But those in whose hearts is perversity follow the part thereof that is allegorical, seeking discord and searching for its hidden meanings, but no one knows its hidden meanings except God. And those who are firmly grounded in knowledge say: "We believe in the Book; the whole of it is from our Lord," and none will grasp the Message except men of understanding. (3:7)

This is the Book in which there is no doubt. In it is guidance to those who fear God, who believe in the unseen, are steadfast in prayer and spend out of what We have provided for them, and who believe in the revelation sent to thee (Muhammad) and sent before thy time, and (in their hearts) have the assurance of the Hereafter. They are on (true) guidance from their Lord, and it is these who will prosper. (2:2-5)

And if you are in doubt as to what We have revealed from time to time to Our servant (Muhammad), then produce a *surah* (chapter of the Qur'an) like thereunto, and call your witnesses or helpers besides God, if your doubts are true. But if you cannot—and of a surety you cannot—then fear the Fire whose fuel is men and stones, which is prepared for those who reject faith. (2:23-24)

READING 3B

Wahy (Revelation)*
MUHAMMAD ABDUL RAUF

And it is not vouchsafed to a mortal that God should speak to him except by revelation or from behind a veil, or by sending a messenger and revealing by His permission what He pleases. Surely He is High, Wise.

And thus did We reveal unto you an inspired Book by Our command. You knew not what the Book was, nor (what) faith (was), but We made it a light, guiding thereby whom We please of Our servants. And surely you guide to the right path. (42:51-52)

The way in which God communicated with His Prophets is called Wahy, i.e., Revelation. This communication between God and His Prophets need not necessarily be in the form of direct speech, but by sending down messages to the Prophets.

One way in which the divine messages reached them was the creation of the sound of the words. The Prophet would hear the words and recognize them to be God's words. It is believed that the Ten Commandments were revealed to Moses on the Mount of Sinai in the same way.

Another type of revelation was by true dreams. The Prophets, being free from complexes that would seek outlets in false dreams, did not suffer from the types of misguiding dreams. Their dreams were therefore true. When they were taught something in

*From Muhammad Abdul Rauf, *Islam Creed and Worship* (Washington, D.C.: The Islamic Center, 1974), pp. 9–10.

their dreams as an instruction from God, they knew that it was a divine revelation. The command given to Abraham to sacrifice his son Ishmael, for example, was given in this form.

The most important form of Wahy was by sending down the divine messages through a special envoy or messenger; namely, the Arch-angel Gabriel who appeared to the Prophets and spoke to them in their own tongues. This was the most important and most effective form of the divine revelation. It was in this form that the Qur'an was revealed to the Prophet Muhammad.

It becomes clear from this discussion that each one of the Prophets received his message fully from God, with no other influence. It is wrong, therefore, to claim, for example, that Moses was in any way influenced by a pre-existing law, or that Jesus or Muhammad borrowed from some earlier religion. Parallels that exist arise from the fact that revealed religions came from the same source and dealt with the same truths.

It is important, however, to bear in mind that the teachings given to the Prophet Muhammad were of two types. One the Prophet conveyed to his followers in his own words. This category is called Hadith.

The second category of revelations given to the Prophet Muhammad consisted not only of ideas but of actual words. The Prophet was commanded to keep the words and to transmit them as they were to his followers. The total message revealed in this form is called the Qur'an. The Qur'an is therefore the word of God. Muhammad merely learned the words from Gabriel and then transmitted them to his disciples. Muslims read the Qur'an as they heard it from the mouth of the Prophet; and subsequent generations read it as each generation heard it from the preceding one. Thus the Qur'an as we read today is the same as was read by the Prophet. It will forever remain as it is, unaltered and untampered with, as God has assured (15:9).

READING 4A
Prophets and Their Virtues*
MUHAMMAD ABDUL RAUF

MEANING OF THE TERM "PROPHET"

In addition to believing in Allah and in His Holy Attributes, we should also believe that He sent some men with His Divine teaching for our guidance. Each one of these men is called Nabi, which means "Prophet". Sometimes, he is called Rasul which means Messenger. The two words are usually used synonymously, but they are sometimes used as two distinct terms. . . .

The first of all Prophets and Messengers was Adam, and the last was Muhammad, peace be upon them all. We believe that all these prophets and messengers were models of good conduct. They possessed all human virtues and were free from all vices.

THE NEED FOR THE PROPHETS

Now an important question arises. Was the advent of these Messengers necessary? In other words, was there any important need for sending these Messengers to mankind? We now proceed to answer this question.

There are many important questions the answers of which we cannot easily reach by ordinary means. There is, for example, the question of the Creator of the world and His nature. Another important question is the ultimate end of the world and the consequences of human deeds. Will the end of people who are

Muslims receive religious instruction in a Turkish mosque.

*From Muhammad Abdul Rauf, *Islam Creed and Worship*, pp. 5–8.

kind and helpful be the same as that of those whose felony causes pain and miseries to millions of people?

Man, as an intellectual being, is inquisitive. He seeks to know the secrets of the universe, and what is hidden behind it. Man craves for the knowledge of how the world was started. Even when man realises that the world must have been created by a Benevolent and Righteous Creator, he further seeks to learn something about the nature of the Creator.

People often wondered, moreover, what end the processes of life would lead to, and what this end would be like. What would be the reward of the righteous, and the fate of the aggressor? Groping in the dark, they arrived at erroneous ideas and developed harmful beliefs and practices. Some worshipped figures like idols and statues, and some were victims of superstitions and magical ideas. . . .

In order to deliver man from the plight of ignorance and from the claws of a superstitious life, God in His grace sent His Prophets to teach man what he needed to know about God and to guide him in the way of worshipping and expressing devotion to God. They also taught us how the end of the world would be, and brought moral teachings for our guidance in life from God Who knows best what is good for us.

Thus there was a great need of divine guidance revealed through the Prophets. They taught the truths about God and the future of man, and laid down the foundations of a model life.

THE CHARACTER OF THE PROPHETS

The great task entrusted to the Prophets could be undertaken only by men of exceptional ability and of perfect character. Therefore, the Prophets were the best of men. They held fast to all virtues, and they were free from serious vices. Muslims, therefore, believe that every one of the Prophets was a model of good behaviour and was of perfect character. . . .

While Muslims believe that all Prophets are to be described generally by all moral perfections, and that they were free from vices, four specific virtues are to be asserted and ascribed to the Prophets, and their opposites are to be denied. These four virtues are:

1. *Sidq,* "Truth", i.e., that they held to the truth. To lie is a grave sin, inconsistent with the integrity of the Prophets.

2. *Amanah,* "Honesty". This virtue means that they were sincere and faithful, and free from all kinds of sins. If they could be sinners and we were to follow them, then sins would become virtues.

3. *Tabligh,* "Transmitting", i.e., that all the Messengers, peace be upon them, conveyed their messages fully without any failure. Concealing their divine message or any part of it would be disobedience and dishonesty, from which they were all free.

4. *Fatanah,* "Intelligence", i.e., that the Prophets were quick-minded and were of the highest degree of intelligence and intellectual ability. Unless they were so highly intelligent, they would not have been able to combat the vehement arguments which were levelled against them by their adversaries.

These four particular virtues of the Prophets; namely, truth, honesty, conveying their messages and intelligence imply that their opposites cannot be ascribed to any of them; namely, telling lies, dishonesty, failure to convey their messages and stupidity.

While Muslims ascribe all human virtues to the Prophets, and deem them free from all vices, they believe that the Prophets were susceptible, like other human beings, to all human needs and crises. None of them appropriated to himself a divine nature or a claim to godship.

WHO ARE THE PROPHETS?

Prophets were sent from the beginning of the human life on earth. The first Prophet was Adam, the father of man, who was created from mud. Many others followed at intervals. The last was Muhammad whose mission started in A.D. 610.

It may be wondered why so many Prophets were sent one after another. In early times, in the absence of permanent records, succeeding generations tended to forget ideas and beliefs transmitted to them by their ancestors, leading to the deterioration of divine teachings. Deliberate corruption by interested individuals and leaders was another factor. Moreover, society in its progress, moving from one stage to another, needed a guidance that would suit the stage of its progress in a given era.

Prophets were therefore sent from time to time to correct the errors and restore the genuine teachings of the faith. Moreover, each mission contained a system for the guidance of people in their human relations as suited their needs.

So we Muslims believe that many Prophets came in the past, but we are not required to determine their number. Twenty-five of these Prophets, however, are mentioned in the Qur'an. . . . Most of these Prophets were also mentioned in the Bible. The Biblical version of most of the names of the Prophets is different from the Arabic version, and they are as follows:

Qur'anic Version	Biblical Version[1]
1. Adam	Adam
2. Nuh	Noah
3. Idris	Enoch
4. Ibrahim	Abraham
5. Isma'il	Ishmael
6. Ishaq	Isaac
7. Ya'qub	Jacob
8. Dawud	David
9. Sulaiman	Solomon
10. Ayyub	Job
11. Yusuf	Joseph
12. Musa	Moses
13. Harun	Aaron
14. Ilyas	Elias
15. Al-Yasa'	Elisha
16. Yunus	Jonah
17. Lut	Lot
18. Hud	
19. Shu'aib	
20. Salih	
21. Dhu'l-kifl	Ezekiel
22. Zakariyya	Zechariah
23. Yahya	John
24. 'Isa	Jesus
25. Muhammad	

Five of these Prophets are given the honorific title Ulu'l-'azm, which means people of determination and perseverance. They are Muhammad, Nuh, Ibrahim, Musa and 'Isa.

[1]Note the absence of Biblical equivalents of some of these names.

READING 4B
The Prophet Muhammad*
SAYYID FAYYAZ MAHMUD

The Prophet's Mosque in Medina, Saudi Arabia.

MUHAMMAD 570–632

The great leader expected and needed by the Arabs appeared at last in Muhammad b. Abdullah b. Abdul Muttalib. He was born in Mecca about the year A.D. 570, to Amina bint Wahb, the wife of Abdullah, son of Abdul Muttalib. Only a few months after the marriage, Abdullah died and Muhammad was born two months after the death of his father. At first, a foster-mother, Halima Saadiya by name, was found for him as was the custom among the aristocrats of those days, but then his mother took charge of him. Unfortunately, she too became ill and died when he was only six years old. Then his grandfather looked after him, but Abdul Muttalib was a very old man and it was not long before that fine old man also died; Muhammad was then nine to ten years old. His uncle, Abu Talib, now took care of him. But little Muhammad was an orphan and must have missed the affection of a father and mother. Despite this unfortunate childhood however, he grew up to be a thoughtful and courteous young man, who was always kind, who showed great generosity of spirit and was invariably tactful and charitable. He spoke the truth, helped others, and was liked by everybody. He had so won the respect of his young contemporaries by the time he was eighteen that they began to call him *al-Amin* ["faithful"].

*From Sayyid Fayyaz Mahmud, *A Short History of Islam* (London: Oxford University Press, 1960), pp. 18–21, 23–27.

YOUTH AND MANHOOD

During his youth, he worked first as a shepherd, then travelled to Palestine and Syria with his uncle Abu Talib, and later managed the business affairs of a wealthy lady of the Quraish, called Khadijah. He was an observant man and kept his eyes open wherever he went; he said little, but heard much. He asked intelligent questions about the why and wherefore of things and pondered over the answers in his own quiet way. But he did not neglect his work, in fact he proved such an intelligent and honest manager that Khadijah offered to marry him. So they were married, Muhammad being then twenty-five years old. Khadijah was his senior by quite a few years, but she was gracious and loving, so they were very happy. After his marriage, Muhammad became economically independent and so had more time to do what he liked best, which was to ponder over things. There were many things to disturb him: the thoughtless ways of the Meccans, the foolish worship of gods and goddesses of the region, beliefs in evil spirits, the evil customs of the land, the intemperate drinking, the excesses of sex, the low estimate of women, the strange practice of some backward tribes of burying baby daughters out of perverse pride, the utter disunity that prevailed, and the bitter feuds. Muhammad pondered over them all, and he was saddened. Life, he thought, was surely not meant to be lived in this way. This was meaningless duplication and an utter waste. There must be a reason for Creation—a meaning and a purpose. There must be an Intelligence behind the world and the larger universe; there must be an answer to the riddle and the answer should be found. He became more and more engrossed in these thoughts. And though he did not cease to be a useful citizen of his beloved Mecca, he began to live an inner life of his own. He started going out of Mecca to sit in a solitary place and devote himself to contemplation. His favourite place was a cave called Hira, which lay in one of the hills outside the old town. He went out more and more by himself, into this lonely place, to think about God and His mysterious ways.

THE REVELATION

Muhammad was now about forty years old. He had observed the practices of other religions and must have heard many people express their views, but he remained dissatisfied. He could never understand how the Arabs, or indeed anybody, could worship so many gods. He was always doubtful, even as a boy, of the wisdom of worshipping stones and spirits. Then one day, whilst he was meditating in the cave, he heard a voice calling his name. He was frightened and returned home quickly. A few days later, the same thing happened, and this time the voice said words which were actually a message from God, the Creator of things. The message had been brought by the Archangel Gabriel and was an annunciation. Muhammad was at first bewildered and he could not believe his senses. He came home troubled and not a little afraid. His wife saw him in this condition and asked him the cause: he told her and then they talked. Gradually his fears abated, but he remained uncertain. It was only after the message had been repeated several times that he was convinced that God had chosen him as a *Nabi* (Prophet). Thereafter he heard from God more and more and spent his time contemplating the Divine Word. It was only after three years that it was finally revealed to him that he was to be a *Rasul* (Messenger) also.

THE RASUL

It was only then that he was asked to preach openly. The messages that he received from Above grew into what we know as the Quran, the sacred book of Islam. Muhammad was asked to preach to his fellowmen, of God's oneness and God's mercy and the duty of man to God. At first, people would not listen to him and he was disheartened, but his wife encouraged him and God sent him heartening messages, and he continued his preachings. There was much opposition, even persecution, but he gradually became so resolved that nothing dismayed him any more. He went about quietly speaking God's Word to whomsoever met him and cared to listen to him. He spoke well, he was a patient teacher, and he was gentle, and people began to listen to him. The words of God charmed people's ears and entered their hearts and many heard him with rapt attention and accepted him. Inevitably there were mockers and scoffers, but slowly the number of believers grew.

EARLY DAYS OF ISLAM

In the beginning, only his wife, his young cousin Ali, and his old friend Abu Bakr believed in him, but then others also stopped to pay heed to his words and his message. He told them of God's bounties, the might and majesty of Allah who had created the earth, the sun, moon, and the stars. He told them that Allah was the only God; Allah gave life and brought death; he was the master of the final day, the day of judgment. He was merciful, though he could be angry with those who were hard and mean and who denied him and worshipped false gods. He enjoined on them to be merciful and kind, he asked them to observe simple virtues. Be charitable to the orphan, the beggar, and the wayfarer, he said. Learn to understand the bounties of God who is your creator and protector. But he always told them to give to others what they received from God. God was bountiful Himself and disliked meanness and smallness of spirit. . . .

OPPOSITION

Many Meccans, especially those occupying positions carrying social or economic prestige, considered Muhammad's words as the rantings of a mad man. They openly scoffed at him, they even abused him. But when they found that instead of being laughed into silence, the Prophet increased his efforts and was listened to attentively by many, they considered it a personal affront. Gradually, they realized that it was a much more serious matter; they began to fear for their positions, especially when they heard that the Prophet was preaching that all Muslims were equal, that they were all like brothers, that God considered that man to be nearest to him who was most pious among men. Being astute politicians, they realized that such words would give birth to a new code of moral and social values. This was definitely a threat to their own superiority, based as it was on birth, social position, on possessions, and worldly goods. So they began to organize determined opposition against the Prophet whom they now openly termed a revolutionary and a danger to the community. They began to work not only against him, but against all the Muslims. Many of these enemies of Islam were rich and strong, so they treated those Muslims badly who were either their slaves or their servants. They beat them when they could, and continually abused them and threatened them; they then boycotted the Prophet. But Muhammad did not believe in returning evil for evil; he asked his followers to be patient. The small Muslim community gained great strength when Omar ibn al Khattab, a prominent and dynamic Meccan, was converted, but even then, the Muslims did not make a large community. The majority of the Meccans were so hostile that the Prophet seriously began to think that those Muslims who could leave Mecca, should go to other countries. Some did go to Habash, the country which is now known as Abyssinia. But that country was too far away. The Muslims who went there found themselves cut off from their own kith and kin and surrounded by unfriendly people.

SOME MEDINITES HEAR MUHAMMAD

To their great good fortune some people from Yathrib (Medina), the other important town of Arabia, came one year to the annual gathering in Mecca and heard the preachings of Muhammad. The Medinites were a sober, unprejudiced people and they heard the Prophet with greater detachment. Free from jealousies or clan rivalries, they gave the Prophet a fair hearing. They were impressed, and when they went back to Medina they decided to tell their townsmen about the new Message. The people of Medina became curious too and they came and heard Muhammad for themselves. They became convinced that the Prophet spoke God's words and, hearing of the difficulties of Muhammad in Mecca, they invited him to come over to Medina. They told him that they would give him every facility to preach in their town and that they would welcome all the emigrants too. They would work with them and for them, and they would fight their enemies with them as if they were their own brothers. They were so sincere in their assurances that the Prophet was persuaded.

THE INVITATION

The Prophet consulted his companions. Did they like the idea of going away to another town? Many did not want to leave their own beloved Mecca, but they knew that their enemies were too strong and that life was not easy for the Prophet and the Muslims in Mecca. They realized that they would be welcomed in Yathrib, and in that town they could live together in peace. The Arab, as we have seen, had always been a wanderer and a journey to another place was not difficult for him. The idea of emigrating to Yathrib was, therefore, not irksome to them. Thus encouraged, Muhammad won over the others who were still doubtful, and a date was fixed for their departure. The Prophet then gave his decision.

THE HIJRAH 622

He asked his followers to go in twos and threes to Medina. They did as he told them. After many of them had left, he too went one night and Abu Bakr, his old friend and companion, went with him. The emissaries of the Meccans pursued them, but Muhammad and Abu Bakr wisely hid in a cave and after a few days, when it was safe, they left quietly for Medina. The Prophet's departure for Medina is a memorable event and its date, July A.D. 622, only ten years before his death, forms the starting point of the Muslim calendar. The event is called the Hijrah which means departure. The Muslims calculate their time from after the Hijrah, called also the Hijrat in Urdu and Persian.

THE FIGHT FOR ISLAM—BADR 624

After the Hijrah, the Muslims, only a few hundred in number, settled down in Medina. Soon all the people of this town accepted the new religion of Islam. They became known as Ansars or the Helpers and they actually grew to be such firm believers that they fought for Islam and their Prophet with the bravest of his followers. Muhammad had to fight many battles in his life and two of his early ones are very famous. The first one was the Battle of Badr, which was fought in the month of Ramazan in A.D. 624. The Muslims under instructions from the Prophet, had intercepted a caravan of the Meccans which was on its way back from Syria under the leadership of Abu Sufyan the Meccan. This was good strategy because Mecca was the head of the opposition as well as the commercial centre of Arabia. To cut the trade route to Syria and the North would weaken the Meccans. The wily Abu Sufyan, however, got wind of the Muslim plans and sent to Mecca for aid, but although the aid arrived, it was of no avail, for the Muslims were led by the Prophet himself and they showed such discipline and such disregard for life that they won a complete victory.

UHUD 625; KHAYBAR 627

The Meccans were greatly mortified, for the defeat was a great blow to their prestige and honour. Moreover blood had been shed and it cried for vengeance. There was furious preparation for war and the Meccans called on their allies. Next year they retaliated by invading Medina, and met the Muslims at the battlefield of Uhud. The Muslim army, disregarding the instructions of the Prophet, grew overbold and began to fight without plan or direction. The result was that the superior army of the Meccans won the day. The Prophet was wounded and the Muslims were so ashamed that they could not look the Prophet in the face. But they did not lose heart and the Prophet took immediate action. The very next day he assembled the Muslims and marched with them in pursuit of the Meccans. When he caught up with them, it was evening, so he encamped and ordered huge fires to be built. The Meccans realized who their pursuers were, but dared not attack the Medinites. The morale of the Muslims, therefore, rose and they rejoiced at this brilliant strategy on the part of the Prophet. Two years later, the Meccans with their allies the Jews again invaded Medina with a large army, but the Prophet had dug a defensive ditch round Medina, so the Meccans besieged the town fruitlessly and after a few exchanges returned discomfited. This battle is called the Battle of the Ditch. Since the Jews had sided with the Meccans, the Prophet now waged war against them. The Jews resisted stoutly in places, but they could not withstand the Prophet, who had grown into a good general by this time, and they were defeated. The last battle against the Jews was the Battle of Khaybar. After this battle, the Jews were offered terms which became the model for later offers to the Dhimmis [nonbelievers in Islamic states]. They were allowed to retain their lands and possessions provided they paid a certain percentage of their produce to the Bait-al-Mal [state treasury] at Medina. It was at this battle that Ali won his spurs, and it was after this battle that a Jewess, Zainab by name, gave poisoned food to the Prophet who, though he spat out the very first morsel, suffered long from its effects.

CONQUEST OF MECCA

In A.D. 628, the Prophet led a large contingent of Muslims to Mecca on the occasion of the annual Hajj pilgrimage, but the Meccans refused to permit such a large body of Muslims into the town. The Muslims, however, stood firm and negotiations were begun and a pact was drawn up, called the Pact of Hudaibiya, which also included a ten years' truce. According to this Pact, the Quraish of Mecca admitted the right of the Prophet to preach to people and convert them, as also the right of the Muslims to perform the Hajj ceremonies every year. It was a diplomatic triumph for the Prophet. From then on, the Bedouin joined the ranks of Islam in large numbers. Two years later, the Meccans having broken the terms, the Prophet led another expedition against Mecca and entered the town as a conqueror, but he was merciful to his old enemies. He, of course, smashed the idols in the Kaaba, purging that holy place for all time of man-made symbols of worship. He then declared in the words of the Quran, "Truth has come and falsehood has vanished, indeed falsehood was bound to go!" But he forgave all his enemies and made a lasting peace with them. Impressed by the Prophet's *mur'uwah* (nobility), the quality most admired by the Arabs, the majority of the Meccans accepted Islam. In the last two years of his life, the Prophet also made peace treaties with the Jewish and Christian tribes to the north. He even established a garrison in the North of Arabia, where the Ghassanids were settled, and received delegations from almost all the Arab tribes of the land. By A.D. 630, Muhammad was accepted by most of the Arabs as the Prophet-king of Arabia and he sent out preachers to all the tribes. It was during this Medinese period, that instructions were received from on high about those fundamental Principles of Life on which the moral and social codes of Islam are based.

A manuscript painting of Muhammad's army en route to Badr. Note that Muhammad's face has not been painted. Islam prohibits pictorial representation of God and of the Prophet as it is believed such art would lead to the worship of idols and icons.

READING 5
Belief in God's Angels*
ABUL ALA MAUDUDI

The Angel Gabriel.

Prophet Muhammad (peace be upon him) has further instructed us to have faith in the existence of God's angels. This . . . article of Islamic faith . . . is very important because it absolves the concept of Tawheed [faith in the Unity of God] from all probable impurities and makes it pure, simple and free from the danger of every conceivable shadow of *shirk* (polytheism).

The polytheists have associated two kinds of creatures with God:

(a) Those which have material existence and are perceptible to the human eye such as sun, moon, stars, fire, water, animals, great men, etc.

(b) Those who have no material existence and are not perceptible to the human eye: the unseen beings who are believed to be engaged in the administration of the universe; for instance, one controls the air, another imparts light, another brings rains and so on and so forth.

The alleged deities of the first kind have material existence and are before the man's eye. The falsity of their claim has been fully exposed by the *Kalima—La ilaha illallah* [that is, by the creed— There is no deity except God]. This is sufficient to dispose of the idea that they enjoy any share in divinity or deserve any reverence at all. The second kind of things, being immaterial as they are, are

*From Abul A'la Maududi, *Towards Understanding Islam*, 9th ed., trans. and ed. by Khurshid Ahmad (Lahore, West Pakistan: Islamic Publications Limited, 1965), pp. 104–7.

hidden from the human eye and are mysterious; the polytheists are more inclined to pin their faith in them. They consider them to be deities, gods and God's children. They make their images and render offerings to them. In order to purify the belief in the unity of God, and to clear it from the admixture of this second kind of unseen creatures, this particular article of faith has been expounded.

Muhammad (God's blessings be upon him) has informed us that these imperceptible spiritual beings, whom people believe to be deities or gods or God's children, are really His angels. They have no share in God's divinity, they are under His command, and are so obedient that they cannot deviate from His commands even to the extent of the slightest fraction of an inch. God employs them to administer His Kingdom, and they carry out His orders exactly and accurately. They have no authority to do anything of their own accord; they cannot present to God any scheme conceived by themselves; they are not authorized even to intercede with God for any man. To worship them, and to solicit their help is degrading and debasing for man. . . .

Muhammad (God's blessings be upon him) forbade us to worship angels, and to associate them with God in His divinity, but along with it he informed us that they were chosen creatures of God, free from sin, from their very nature unable to disobey God, and ever engaged in carrying out His orders. Moreover, he informed us that these angels of God surround you from all sides, are attached to you, and are always in your company. They observe and note all your actions, good or bad. They preserve complete record of every man's life. After death when you will be brought before God, they will present a full report of your life-work on earth, wherein you will find everything correctly recorded, not a single movement left out, howsoever insignificant and howsoever carefully concealed it may be.

We have not been informed of the intrinsic nature of the angels. Only some of their virtues or attributes have been mentioned to us, and we have been asked to believe in their existence. We have no other means of knowing their nature, their attributes, and their qualities. It would be, therefore, sheer folly on our part to attribute any form or quality to them on our accord. We must believe in them exactly as we have been asked to do. To deny their existence is *kufr* for, firstly, we have no reason for such a denial, and, secondly, our denial of them would be tantamount to attributing untruth to Muhammad (God's blessings be upon him). We believe in their existence only because God's true Messenger has informed us of it.

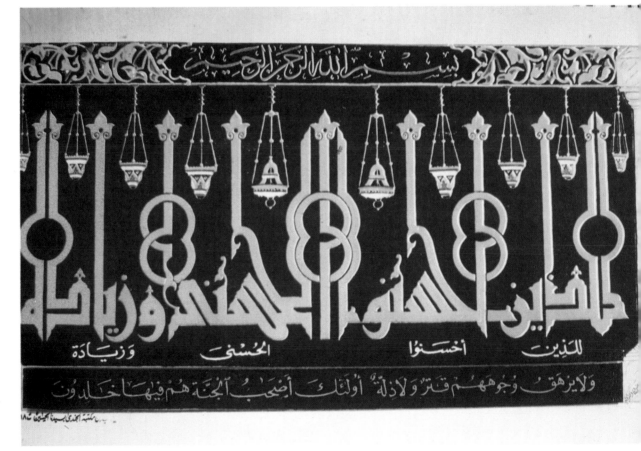

Part of a manuscript in decorative Arabic script that says, "For those who have done good, there will be good (in the Hereafter) and more. . . ."

READING 6

The Hereafter*
ZEBA SIDDIQUI

Concerning life after death, the Holy Qur'an says:

> Verily, We shall give life to the dead, and We record that which they send before and that which they leave behind, and of all things have We taken account in a clear book (of evidence). (36:12)

> And to every soul will be paid in full the fruit of its deeds, and God knows best all that they do. (39:70)

The Qur'an, as well as the earlier revelations sent by God, teaches that human beings are accountable to God, and that the Hereafter, not this world, is the final goal of all. If people follow God's guidance, they will attain good in this world and in the Hereafter. If not, although they may appear to prosper in this brief earthly existence, they will lose all spiritual good and will suffer the results of disobedience to God in the life to come. This is a spiritual law just as certain as the laws which govern the physical world. For this world is temporal. It will end one day, at a time known only to God. On that Day of Judgment, all human beings will be raised in physical form and brought before God to give an accounting of their intentions and deeds.

God's justice and mercy are equally impartial and perfect, and no one will be wronged in the slightest degree in this judgment:

> Then anyone who has done an atom's weight of good shall see it, and anyone who has done an atom's weight of evil shall see it. (99:7–8)

---

*From Zeba Siddiqui, "This Is Islam" (to be published by the Muslim Students' Association of the United States and Canada).

Those who have earned punishment will suffer in proportion to the evil they have done, while those who have earned good will be in a state of bliss.[1] These two states, Heaven and Hell (*Jannat* and *Jahannum* in Arabic), are not merely spiritual or mental states; they will be experienced physically as well.

The Qur'an states that in Heaven people will experience some things which will remind them of their life on earth, and its happiness and beauty will far exceed anything they can imagine. The ultimate triumph and joy for those who have attained Heaven will be the nearness to their Lord. As for those who have deserved Hell, theirs will be a temporary or permanent state of torture, depending on the nature and extent of their sins. The Qur'an describes this torture as intense physical burning and agony, heightened by the terrible knowledge that they brought this fate on themselves by persistently rejecting the guidance that God had given them.

The Holy Qur'an says:

Does not man see that it is We Who created him from sperm? Yet behold, he stands forth as an open adversary. And he makes comparisons for us, and forgets his own creation. He says, "Who can give life to (dry) bones and decomposed ones?" Say (O Muhammad): "He will give them life Who created them for the first time, for He is well versed in every kind of creation. . . . Is not He Who created the heavens and the earth able to create the like thereof?" Yes, indeed, for He is the Creator Supreme, of infinite skill and knowledge. Verily, when He intends a thing, His command is "Be," and it is. Then glory to Him in Whose hands is the dominion of all things, and to Him will you all be brought back. (36:77–79, 81–83)

Every soul shall have a taste of death, and only on the Day of Judgment shall you be paid your full recompense. Only he who is saved far from the Fire (of Hell) and admitted to the Garden (Heaven) will have attained the object (of life), for the life of this world is but a thing that deceives. (3:185)

Verily God will admit those who believe and do righteous deeds to Gardens beneath which rivers flow, while those who reject God will enjoy (this world) and eat as cattle eat, and the Fire will be their abode. (47:12)

[1]For descriptions of Hell in the Qur'an, see 43:74–77, 67:6–12, 84:1–15, and many others. For Heaven, see 3:15, 198; 10:9–10; 50:31–35; 57:21, and many others.

READING 7
Qadar*
HAMMUDAH ABDALATI

The true Muslim believes in the timeless knowledge of God and in His power to plan and execute His plans. God is not indifferent to this world nor is He neutral to it. His knowledge and power are in action at all times to keep order in His vast domain and maintain full command over His creation. He is Wise and Loving, and whatever He does must have a good motive and a meaningful purpose. If this is established in our minds, we should accept with good Faith all that He does, although we may fail to understand it fully, or even think it is bad. We should have strong Faith in Him and accept whatever He does because our knowledge is limited and our thinking is based on individual or personal considerations, whereas His knowledge is limitless and He plans on a universal basis.

This does not in any way make man fatalist or helpless. It simply draws the demarcation line between what is God's concern and what is man's responsibility. Because we are by nature finite and limited, we have a finite and limited degree of power and freedom. We cannot do everything, and He graciously holds us responsible only for the things we do. The things which we cannot do, or things which He Himself does, are not in the realm of our responsibility. He is Just and has given us limited power to match our finite nature and limited responsibility. On the other hand, the

*From Hammudah Abdalati, *Islam in Focus* (Indianapolis, Ind.: American Trust Publications, 1975), pp. 14–15.

timeless knowledge and power of God to execute His plans do not prevent us from making our own plans in our own limited sphere of power. On the contrary, He exhorts us to think, to plan and to make sound choices, but if things do not happen the way we wanted or planned them, we should not lose Faith or surrender ourselves to mental strains and shattering worries. We should try again and again, and if the results are not satisfactory, then we know that we have tried our best and cannot be held responsible for the results, because what is beyond our capacity and responsibility is the affair of God alone. The Muslims call this article of Faith the belief in 'Qadaa' and 'Qadar', which simply means, in other words, that the Timeless Knowledge of God anticipates events, and that events take place according to the exact Knowledge of God (Qur'an, for example, 18:29; 41:46; 53:33–62; 54:49; 65:3; 76:30–31).

A Senegalese Muslim makes a string of beads for prayer.

PART II

The Pillars of Islam

Islam prescribes certain forms of worship for Muslims, as set forth in the Holy Qur'an and exemplified in the practice (Sunnah) of Prophet Muhammad. These acts of worship are known as the Five Pillars of Islam. They are summarized in the following Hadith (saying of the Prophet).

> *Islam is based on five things: the testimony that there is no deity except God and that Muhammad is His servant and messenger* (Shahadah), *the observance of prayer* (Salat), *the payment of* Zakat, *the pilgrimage* (Hajj), *and the fast during Ramadan* (Siyam).

The first of the Pillars is the creed, or declaration of faith (Shahadah). *This creed—*La ilaha illa Allah, Muhammadur Rasul Allah *("There is no deity except God, Muhammad is the Messenger of God")—has already been discussed in Reading 1. It should be pointed out, however, that this declaration means more than the English words convey. It means that Muslims do not love or worship anything other than God. This refers not only to idols but to any philosophies, ideas, life-styles, or desires. Similarly, the second part of the creed is more than a statement of belief in Muhammad as God's Messenger. It is a proclamation of belief in the Prophet's guidance and a statement of the desire to follow that guidance.*

Since the creed requires no further discussion, the readings in this part focus on the last four Pillars of Islam. Note, however, that the Pillars of Islam, like the Articles of Faith, do not follow a prescribed order.

The front (top) and back (bottom) of an eighteenth-century Turkish disc designed to find the direction of Mecca from any given spot. The front is a map with a movable pointer fixed at Mecca. The back is a depiction of Mecca.

READING 8
Prayer*

INTRODUCTION

Among the Five Pillars of Islam, Prayer *(Salat)* is the second, the first being the declaration of Faith *(Shahadah)*. Fasting *(Siyam)* is observed for one month each year, the Poor-due *(Zakat)* is given once a year, and the Pilgrimage *(Hajj)* is performed once in a lifetime, but prayers *(salat)* are five times a day—at dawn, in the early afternoon, in the late afternoon, just after sunset, and at night. The essence of Islam is consciousness of and submission to God, and the most direct means of developing these qualities is through prayer. It is clear that prayer once a week or even once a day is not enough, as we become so absorbed in our activities that we tend to forget our Creator. That is why prayers are prescribed five times each day.

It may seem difficult at times to observe all the prayers regularly, but to those who are humble before their Creator and who believe that they shall meet Him after death, it is a joy and a pleasure. This is expressed in Qur'an thus:

> Seek help in patience and prayer. This is indeed hard except to those who are humble, who bear in mind that they shall meet their Lord and that they are to return to Him. (2:45–46)

*Adapted and abridged from Islamic Correspondence Course, Unit 3 (Plainfield, Ind.: The Muslim Students' Association of the United States and Canada, 1974).

The Islamic prayers, like any prayers, have a certain form, a series of actions and recitations, and this has a significance which will be discussed later. But the motions and the words are not the essence of the prayers. The essence of the prayers, indeed of all forms of Islamic worship (Poor-due, Fasting, Pilgrimage), is the spirit of humility and submission to God. This spirit may not be present every time we pray, but with or without it, we should observe all the prayers. It is obvious that if one never prays or prays only seldom, he is not likely to attain the spirit of submission. In fact, the neglect of prayer gradually leads one to feel and to act as if he does not believe in God or in the life hereafter, although he may profess otherwise. On the other hand, one who starts observing prayers regularly may attain, by degrees and stages, a feeling of being present before his Lord, a sense of peace in his heart, a firm criterion of right and wrong in his attitudes and actions, and the spirit of true submission. He will never lose sight of the fact that he is only a human being of limited capacities, living on this earth for a short while, and that his Lord is the Almighty Creator and Sustainer of the universe, Who gave him his life and to Whom he will return. He will become watchful not to go beyond the limits set by God, and he will develop whatever is good in himself and suppress his wrong inclinations and wishes. In time, he should attain such a sharp criterion of good and evil that all his actions follow, in an easy and natural way, whatever is good, noble and worth striving for.

These statements are only an elaboration of what is said to us in Qur'an about prayers:

> O you who believe! seek help with patient perseverance and prayer; for God is with those who patiently persevere. (2:153)

> Those who believe, and whose hearts find satisfaction in the remembrance of God: for without doubt by the remembrance of God hearts are refreshed. (13:28)

> Establish regular prayers—at the sun's decline till the darkness of the night, and the recitation of the dawn prayer: surely the recitation of the dawn prayer is witnessed. And as for the night, keep vigil a part of it, as a work of supererogation [doing more than duty requires] for thee: it may be that thy Lord will raise thee up to a praiseworthy station. (17:78–79)

> . . . and proclaim the praises of thy Lord before the rising of the sun, and before its setting; and proclaim thy Lord's praises in the

Performing wudu *outside a Moroccan mosque.*

watches of the night, and at the ends of the day: that thou mayest have (spiritual) joy. (20:130)

So glory be to God, when you reach eventide and when you rise at dawn—His is the praise in the heavens and on earth—and in the late afternoon when the day begins to decline. (30:17-18)

And be steadfast in prayer and regular in charity: and whatever good you send forth for your souls before you, you shall find it with God: for God sees well all that you do. (2:110)

It should be borne in mind that God does not need our prayers, for He is above all needs. God's authority over the universe, including all human affairs, is not decreased in the least even if no man acknowledges Him or prays to Him. He does not require our prostrations or our words of praise to add to His majesty and glory. The prayers are for ourselves, for our own spiritual good, in harmony with our own natural instinct to proclaim God's glory and to bow down before Him in thankfulness and praise.

The Islamic form of prayer achieves these instinctive aspirations to the utmost extent. We wash ourselves (wudu), which not only cleans and refreshes us but also prepares us mentally for the act of prayer. We stand before God, seeking His guidance and help, and ask Him again and again to show us the straight path. We recite from His Book and refresh our belief in His mercy and goodness, in the fact that we will one day return to Him to give an accounting of ourselves, in the moral teachings of Qur'an and in the truth of His messenger Muhammad (peace be on him). The bowing and prostration are the very embodiment of the spirit of humility and submission to God.

Prayers are also an expression of brotherhood and equality among men. In a congregational prayer, we stand shoulder to shoulder with our fellow-worshippers, without distinction of social or economic status, race or color, and perform with the leader the various movements, prostrating ourselves together as one body before God. This creates among Muslims a bond of love and mutual respect which transcends all worldly considerations.

We perform the sequence of actions and recitations, both in our ablutions and in our prayers, in the way in which our Prophet (peace be on him) performed them. All Muslims throughout the world pray in the same manner in which the Prophet prayed, thus witnessing to the fact that all Muslims are one community, the community of God and His messenger.

We will now describe the actual form in which prayers are performed.

ABLUTION (WUDU) AND DRY CLEANSING (TAYAMMUM)

Before our prayers, we wash the exposed parts of our bodies, first silently saying that our intention in washing is to make *wudu,* in the following sequence: (1) wash hands three times; (2) rinse mouth three times; (3) clean nostrils three times by sniffing in and blowing out water from one cupped hand; (4) wash face with both hands three times; (5) wash arms up to the elbow three times, the right arm before the left; (6) wipe top of head with wet hands, ears with thumb and forefinger, and neck with backs of wet hands once; (7) wash feet up to ankles three times, right foot first. When the *wudu* is completed, we are ready for prayers.

It is not necessary to make ablution *(wudu)* for every prayer unless during the interval between two prayers you have performed any toilet function, passed gas, vomited or slept. In these cases a repetition of *wudu* is required before your next prayer. It is also not necessary to wash your feet again if you had on socks or stockings after the first *wudu* of the day, but the feet are to be washed once a day for prayers.

In case of sickness in which it would be harmful to use water or when water is scarce or not available, you can substitute a dry cleansing *(tayammum)* for ablution. For *tayammum,* you strike your hands lightly on a clean wall or on clean earth or sand, and wipe your face with them once. Then you again strike your hands on the clean surface and wipe each arm up to the elbow once, right arm first. This is a symbolic act of conforming to God's ordinance of cleanliness as a condition for prayers and again has the effect of preparing ourselves mentally for prayers.

All these practices are performed in keeping with the *Sunnah* (Practices) of the Prophet (peace be on him) or, in the case of women, according to the Prophet's instructions.

DRESS

For prayers the Prophet (peace be on him) enjoined that men and boys should be covered at least from the navel to the knee. The head may be covered or uncovered, and the shoes are always removed. For women, the Prophet recommended that they should be covered from head to foot, leaving only the face and hands uncovered. This is sometimes difficult to do in Western dress, but one should try. Some Muslim ladies have found it practical and appropriate to wear for prayers a wide shawl or piece of cloth (roughly 2½ yards long and 54 inches wide) which can be draped over the head to make a secure covering for the head and body. Others have found it convenient to wear slacks under their dresses, together with a covering for the head, for prayers.

A CLEAN PLACE

We want to ensure that the place where we will pray will be reasonably clean, and it is desirable (but not essential) to provide some sort of covering, at least for the spot where our foreheads will touch the floor or ground during prostration. A napkin, handkerchief, towel, sheet or small rug will suffice for this purpose. In Muslim countries rugs are available for prayers, but this is only a matter of convenience, not of necessity.

THE PRAYERS (SALAT)

Before going through the complete sequence of the prayers, there are three things to bear in mind:

A. Each of the five daily prayers consists of either two, three or four units *(rakat)*, which will be described later.
B. The names of the five daily prayers, their times and the number of units *(rakat)* in each are as follows:
   1. *Fajr* (the dawn prayer), to be observed some time between dawn and sunrise, consists of two units *(rakat)*, both of which are said *aloud.*
   2. *Zuhr* (the early afternoon prayer), to be observed some time just after noon until mid-afternoon, consists of four *rakat,* all of which are said *silently.*
   3. *'Asr* (the late afternoon prayer), to be observed some time between mid-afternoon and sunset, consists of four *rakat,* all of which are said *silently.*
   4. *Maghrib* (the evening prayer), to be observed some time just after sunset until the last light fades, consists of three *rakat,*

of which the first two are said *aloud* and the third is said *silently.*

5. *'Isha* (the night prayer), to be observed at some time during the night, consists of four *rakat,* of which the first two are said *aloud* and the last two *silently.*

C. There are four basic positions which we assume during our prayers.

1. *Standing (qiyam),* with the right hand clasped lightly above the left, wrist over wrist, and held a little above the waist.
2. *Bowing (ruku),* with the hands placed just above the knees.
3. *Prostrating (sujud),* with the forehead and tip of the nose touching the floor, the hands with fingers spread out slightly resting on the floor, and elbows slightly raised.
4. *Sitting (julus),* with legs folded under the body.

The positions of qiyam *and* ruku.

Before beginning the prayer, we ascertain the direction of Ka'bah *(Qibla),* the first house of worship of One God, built by Abraham in Mecca (in what is now Saudi Arabia). This is East, North-East or South-East in the United States and Canada.

Placing the covering we have provided on the floor in front of us, we stand straight, facing the direction of Ka'bah and silently say that we intend to pray two (or three or four) *rakat* of obligatory *Fajr* (or *Zuhr, 'Asr, Maghrib* or *'Isha,* as the case may be) for the sake of God.

Now we raise our hands to our ears, saying *aloud,* "God is Most Great."[1]

We then place our hands wrist over wrist and *silently* recite our Praise *(Thana):*

Glory be to Thee, O God, and Thine is the praise,
and blessed is Thy name,
and exalted is Thy majesty,
and there is none worthy of worship except Thee.

I take refuge in God from Satan the rejected.

The last line of this prayer means that we intend in our prayer only to worship God, not to be diverted to other thoughts, and that we seek refuge in God against all temptation.

Remaining in this position, we now recite the opening *surah* (chapter) of Qur'an, starting in the name of God.

[1]Only the English translation of the prayers in this reading is given. Note, however, that these prayers are recited in Arabic in actual worship.

In the name of God, the Merciful, the Mercy-giving.

All praise is due to God, Lord of the Worlds,
the Merciful, the Mercy-giving,
Master of the Day of Judgment.
Thee alone do we worship and from Thee alone do ask help.
Show us the straight path,
the path of those upon whom is Thy favor,
who have not deserved Thy anger,
and who have not gone astray. Amen.

Now, in the same posture, we recite a short passage or one of the short *surahs* (chapters) from Qur'an.

Now we bow with our hands just above our knees, and again say *aloud,* "God is Most Great," and then, in this position, we say *silently* three times, "Glory be to my Lord, the Almighty."

We then stand erect for a moment and say *aloud* once, "God hears those who call upon Him," and then *silently* once, "Our Lord, praise be to Thee."

Saying *aloud* "God is Most Great," we now prostrate and in this position say *silently* three times, "Glory be to my Lord, the Most High."

Saying *aloud* "God is Most Great," we lift ourselves to a sitting posture for a moment's rest before the next prostration, and again saying *aloud* "God is Most Great," we again prostrate and again say silently three times, "Glory be to my Lord, the Most High."

This completes one unit *(rakat)* of the prayer.

The second *rakat* will be exactly like the first except that after the second prostration, we will again assume the sitting posture and *silently* say our *Declaration (Tashahud):*

All service, all worship and all sanctity are for God.
Peace be upon you, O Prophet, and God's mercy and blessings.
Peace be upon us and upon those who practice righteousness.
I bear witness that there is no deity but God,
and I bear witness that Muhammad is His servant and messenger.

If this is a two-*rakat* prayer *(Fajr),* we will say in addition here the prayer known as *Salatul Ibraheemiyah* (Ibraheemi Prayer, referring to Abraham).

O God, exalt Muhammad and the family of Muhammad

as Thou hast exalted Abraham and the family of Abraham,
and bless Muhammad and the family of Muhammad

as Thou hast blessed Abraham and the family of Abraham.
Thou art the Praised, the Glorious.

In a two-*rakat* prayer, after we have finished this recitation, we turn our faces, first to the right side, saying, "Peace be upon you and God's blessings," and then we turn our faces to the left side, saying again, "Peace be upon you and God's blessings."

This completes a two-*rakat* prayer, i.e., *Fajr*.

The remaining four prayers of the day have four *(Zuhr)*, four *('Asr)*, three *(Maghrib)* and four *('Isha) rakat* respectively.

SUPEREROGATORY OR ADDITIONAL (SUNNAH) PRAYERS

It was the practice of the Prophet (peace be on him) often to say additional prayers immediately preceding and/or following the prescribed prayers which we have just described. The *prescribed* prayers are called *Fard* and the *additional* prayers are called *Sunnah* prayers.

Sunnah prayers are *recommended,* in distinction to the *Fard* prayers, which are obligatory.

PERSONAL PRAYER OR SUPPLICATION (DU'A)

Upon the completion of the required *(Fard)* prayers or the *Sunnah* prayers if they are said, we find time and opportunity to pray to God in our own words *(du'a)* if we wish, expressing whatever is in our hearts, whether it be praise, thanksgiving, asking for forgiveness, supplication for ourselves or for others, or any other thing. This is said sitting, immediately after the formal prayer is over, with the hands held up next to each other, palms up and fingers slightly curled. However, this is optional, not a required or essential part of any prayer. It should be borne in mind that in Islam there is no limit on how often or how much one prays personal prayer *(du'a)* apart from the regular prayers *(salat)* five times each day.

UNUSUAL CIRCUMSTANCES

There are many circumstances in which it is not possible to observe prayers in exactly the manner described here. If one is sick, for instance, one can make dry cleansing instead of ablution with water and can pray the entire prayer sitting in the described sitting posture, moving the hands at the proper times to follow the motions, or one can sit instead of standing and bowing but then can perform the prostrations from the sitting posture. If necessary, one can pray lying in bed. When travelling, it is desirable to stop for prayers if possible, but if it is difficult or impossible, one can pray just as one is sitting in the bus, train, plane, etc., moving the hands as usual to follow the motions. In addition, permission is given in Qur'an to shorten the prayers, while travelling, to two rakat for each prayer.

It is permitted to combine prayers if it is not possible to observe one prayer at the proper time. This is appropriate only when we truly are not able to observe some prayer within the proper time limits, but not as a way to avoid the obligation of prayer at regular times five times each day. However, it is our obligation to make up later for any prayer which is not observed at the proper time, whatever the reasons.

CONGREGATIONAL PRAYERS

It is recommended that when two or more Muslims are present at the time of a prayer they form a congregation and pray together. A leader *(imam)* is selected from among the men in the group, preferably a person of religious knowledge and piety. The leader stands in front by himself, while the rest of the group form straight parallel rows behind him, standing shoulder to shoulder but not touching each other, all facing *Qibla* (the direction of Ka'bah). Women form separate parallel rows behind the men. The whole prayer is performed in the same manner as any individual prayer, with the worshippers following the leader in his movements without preceding him in any act.

THE CALL TO PRAYERS (ADHAN)

If one is praying individually, the call to prayers *(adhan)* is not necessary, although one may give it if he wishes. But for a congregational prayer, *adhan* is given so that the Muslims may know that it is prayer time and assemble at the place of worship. The caller *(muezzin)* stands facing *Qibla* (the direction of Mecca) and with his hands raised to his ears chants in a loud voice:

Jordanian Muslims in congregational prayer.

God is Most Great, God is Most Great, God is Most
   Great, God is Most Great.
I bear witness that there is no deity but God, I
   bear witness that there is no deity but God.
I bear witness that Muhammad is a messenger of God,
   I bear witness that Muhammad is a messenger of God.
Come to prayer, come to prayer.
Come to your good, come to your good.
God is Most Great, God is Most Great.
There is no deity but God.

When the *adhan* is given for *Fajr* (dawn) prayer, the following sentence is inserted between the fifth and sixth lines: "Prayer is better than sleep, prayer is better than sleep."

After *adhan* is called, the worshippers gather at the place of prayer, and when they are assembled, a second call, known as *iqamah* (summons), is recited by one of the congregation. This is identical to the *adhan,* except that it is recited faster and not as loudly, and the following sentence is added between the fifth and sixth lines: "Stand for prayers, stand for prayers."

FRIDAY (JUM'A) PRAYER

Apart from the five daily prayers, the Friday *(Jum'a)* congregational prayer is obligatory upon Muslim men and boys. Women, due to their household responsibilities, are excused from the obligation of praying *Jum'a* prayer in congregation and can pray *Zuhr* prayer at home as usual. However, if it is possible and convenient, they may join in the congregational *Jum'a* prayer.

THE MONTH OF FASTING

9—RAMADAN 1397

(AUGUST 16—SEPTEMBER 14, 1977)

DAYS	DATES A.H. 1397 RAMADAN	DATES A.D. 1977 AUGUST	MAGHRIB SUNSET P.M. hrs. min.	ISHA NIGHT P.M. hrs. min.	SAHOOR LAST MEAL A.M. hrs. min.	IMSAK STOP EAT A.M. hrs. min.	FAJR DAWN A.M. hrs. min.	SHURUQ SUNRISE A.M. hrs. min.	ZUHR NOON P.M. hrs. min.	ASR AFTERNOON P.M. hrs. min.
TUE*	1	16	8 02	9 42	2 14	4 14	4 34	6 22	1 12	4 59
WED	2	17	8 01	9 40	2 15	4 15	4 35	6 23	1 12	4 58
THU	3	18	7 59	9 38	2 16	4 16	4 36	6 24	1 12	4 57
FRI	4	19	7 58	9 36	2 18	4 18	4 38	6 25	1 11	4 57
SAT	5	20	7 56	9 34	2 19	4 19	4 39	6 26	1 11	4 56
SUN	6	21	7 55	9 33	2 20	4 20	4 40	6 26	1 11	4 55
MON	7	22	7 53	9 31	2 22	4 22	4 42	6 27	1 11	4 55
TUE	8	23	7 52	9 29	2 23	4 23	4 43	6 28	1 10	4 54
WED	9	24	7 50	9 27	2 24	4 24	4 44	6 29	1 10	4 53
THU	10	25	7 49	9 25	2 25	4 25	4 45	6 30	1 10	4 52
FRI	11	26	7 48	9 23	2 26	4 26	4 46	6 31	1 10	4 51
SAT	12	27	7 46	9 21	2 28	4 28	4 48	6 32	1 09	4 51
SUN	13	28	7 45	9 20	2 29	4 29	4 49	6 32	1 09	4 50
MON	14	29	7 43	9 18	2 30	4 30	4 50	6 33	1 09	4 49
TUE	15	30	7 42	9 16	2 32	4 32	4 52	6 34	1 09	4 49

*Fasting begins at 4:14 a.m. on Tuesday.

Note: 1. Period of fasting starts from pre-dawn (as indicated above by "Imsak") and lasts until sunset.

2. The five major times for prayer are (1) early morning (Fajr), (2) early afternoon (Zuhr), (3) late afternoon (Asr), (4) early after sunset (Maghrib), and (5) late after sunset (Isha).

3. This time table of prayers and fasting was specially prepared by the Islamic Center for Washington, D.C. Muslims living outside the Metropolitan area should take into consideration the difference in time.

DAYS	DATES		TIMES OF PRAYERS								
	A.H. 1397 RAMADAN	A.D. 1977 AUGUST	MAGHRIB SUNSET P.M. hrs. min.	ISHA NIGHT P.M. hrs. min.	SAHOOR LAST MEAL A.M. hrs. min.	IMSAK STOP EAT A.M. hrs. min.	FAJR DAWN A.M. hrs. min.	SHURUQ SUNRISE A.M. hrs. min.	ZUHR NOON P.M. hrs. min.	ASR AFTERNOON P.M. hrs. min.
WED	16	31	7 40	9 14	2 33	4 33	4 53	6 35	1 08	4 48
THU	17	SEP. 1	7 39	9 12	2 34	4 34	4 54	6 36	1 08	4 47
FRI	18	2	7 38	9 10	2 35	4 35	4 55	6 37	1 08	4 46
SAT	19	3	7 36	9 08	2 36	4 36	4 56	6 38	1 07	4 45
SUN	20	4	7 35	9 07	2 37	4 37	4 57	6 38	1 07	4 44
MON	21	5	7 33	9 05	2 39	4 39	4 59	6 39	1 07	4 43
TUE	22	6	7 32	9 03	2 40	4 40	5 00	6 40	1 06	4 42
WED	23	7	7 30	9 01	2 41	4 41	5 01	6 41	1 06	4 41
THU	24	8	7 29	8 59	2 42	4 42	5 02	6 42	1 06	4 40
FRI	25	9	7 27	8 57	2 43	4 43	5 03	6 42	1 05	4 39
SAT	26	10	7 26	8 56	2 44	4 44	5 04	6 43	1 05	4 38
SUN*	27	11	7 24	8 54	2 45	4 45	5 05	6 44	1 05	4 37
MON	28	12	7 23	8 52	2 46	4 46	5 06	6 45	1 04	4 36
TUE	29	13	7 21	8 50	2 48	4 48	5 08	6 46	1 04	4 35
WED†	30	14	7 20	8 49	2 49	4 49	5 09	6 46	1 04	4 34

*The day following Lailatul-Qadr
†The last day of fasting

A beggar in Casablanca, Morocco. The more affluent Muslims develop a greater sympathy for the suffering of the poor as a result of fasting.

READING 9
Fasting*

Fasting *(Siyam)* is an act of pure submission to God's command, given in the Qur'an, to observe the fast. Fasting has many benefits, which we will discuss presently, but its true significance is to develop a sense of complete obedience to the One Who created us and gave us our physical and spiritual needs and the means to fulfill these needs. We acknowledge that God is our Sustainer, and through His bounty—through the use of natural resources and our faculties—we obtain our sustenance. Hence, if God commands us to abstain from food, drink and the fulfillment of other natural appetites for a period of time, we gladly obey His command. God says in Qur'an:

> O you who believe! Fasting is ordained for you as it was ordained for those before you, so that you may remain conscious of God. (2:183)

While many benefits come to us through fasting the primary benefit is that we learn self-restraint, discipline of our appetites, and flexibility of our habits. Over-indulgence in eating, drinking, smoking or marital relations makes one the slave of his desires and habits. Through fasting one becomes free of this slavery. Through fasting those who are well-off learn to appreciate the afflictions of the poor—hunger and thirst—and become more sympathetic toward them. When a person fasts, he feels that he is

*Adapted from Islamic Correspondence Course, Unit 4 (Plainfield, Ind.: The Muslim Students' Association of the United States and Canada, 1974).

joining the whole Muslim world in a spiritual act, thus increasing his sense of community and brotherhood. Some benefits to a person's health also result from fasting, such as the elimination of fatty substances from the blood, a decrease in the harmful activity of intestinal microbes and of uric acid, and so on. But it should be emphasized that all these benefits are not the object of fasting. As was stated earlier, we fast solely because God commands us to do so, as devout and obedient servants to His will.

Prophet Muhammad (peace be on him) is reported to have said:

> He who fasts during Ramadan with faith and seeking reward from God will have his past sins forgiven.
> Fasting is a shield (against acts of disobedience in this world and against the fire in the next).

RAMADAN—THE MONTH OF FASTING

Ramadan is the ninth month of the Islamic calendar, which is based on the orbiting of the moon (lunar calendar) rather than on the orbiting of the earth (solar calendar). We will comment on this a little later. Here we will discuss the significance of the month of Ramadan, chosen by God for Muslims as the month of fasting. Almighty God says in Qur'an:

> It was in the month of Ramadan that the Qur'an was (first) revealed as guidance unto man and a self-evident proof of that guidance, and as the standard by which to discern the true from the false. Hence, whoever of you is present (at home) shall fast throughout it. (2:185)

Thus, Ramadan is the month in which every single day is a day of fasting.

THE NIGHT OF POWER

The night in which Prophet Muhammad (peace be on him) first received the Divine message through the agency of the Angel Gabriel is referred to in the Qur'an as "The Night of Power" *(Lailat-ul-Qadr)*. It is not known exactly which night of Ramadan is the Night of Power, but according to sound traditions of the Prophet *(Hadith)*, it is one of the odd-numbered nights of the last ten days of Ramadan. In some Muslim countries the night preceding the twenty-seventh day of Ramadan is observed as the

Night of Power, but one cannot be sure about this date. In Qur'an it is said about this Night:

> We have indeed revealed this (Qur'an) in the Night of Power. And what would explain to thee the significance of the Night of Power? The Night of Power is better than a thousand months. Therein descend the angels and the Spirit [Gabriel] by God's permission, on every errand. Peace—until the day breaks. (97:1-5)

The Holy Prophet (peace be on him) is reported to have said: "When the Night of Power comes, Gabriel descends with a company of angels who invoke blessings on everyone who is standing or sitting and remembering the Most Great and Glorious God."

'Aisha, the Prophet's wife, said that God's messenger Muhammad (peace be on him) used to exert himself in devotion during the last ten nights of Ramadan to a greater extent than at any other time.

THE BATTLE OF BADR

An event of great historical importance for Muslims took place during Ramadan. The Battle of Badr was fought on the 17th of Ramadan in the year 2 A.H. (After *Hijra*). It marked the first open struggle between the newly-organized Islamic community in Medina and the enemies of Islam, the pagans of Mecca. The Muslims were outnumbered three to one, were poorly equipped and inexperienced in warfare, but under the inspiring leadership of the Prophet (peace be on him), they fought with courage and valor, and God granted them victory.

THE ISLAMIC LUNAR CALENDAR

It may be noted that all religious observances in Islam are based on the lunar rather than the solar calendar, and there is a significance in this. For example, let us consider Ramadan. Since the lunar year consists of 354 days, it is eleven days (twelve days in a leap year) shorter than the solar year. The month of Ramadan thus rotates gradually through all the seasons—winter, fall, summer and spring. In winter the days are short and cold and fasting is easiest, while in summer the long, hot days make fasting more difficult, and fall and spring bring an intermediate situation. Thus Muslims, whether they live in the Northern or the Southern Hemisphere, become accustomed to fasting in all seasons, sometimes with greater ease and sometimes with greater hardship. If, however, the period of fasting had been fixed in a particular season—say winter in the Northern Hemisphere while it was summer in the Southern Hemisphere—it would have resulted in perpetual ease for one group of Muslims, while the other group suffered perpetual hardship.

Furthermore, a new moon can be sighted by a nomad in the desert and a settler in the town alike, by one who can read calendars and by one who is totally illiterate, and no precise knowledge of the reckoning of dates and days is necessary. In addition, the sighting of the new moon, especially that of Ramadan and that of Shawwal (month following Ramadan), provides great excitement in itself.

KINDS OF FASTING

A. Obligatory

Fasting in Ramadan is obligatory on every Muslim man and woman, with a few exceptions to be mentioned later. Any day of Ramadan on which one does not fast should be made up on a later date.

B. Supererogatory (Additional)

This includes fasts on specific days of the year, such as any six days of Shawwal [tenth month of Islamic calendar], the 9th, 10th and 11th of Muharram [first month], the 15th of Shaban [eighth month], etc. These are recommended and practiced by the Prophet *(sunnah)* but are not obligatory.

C. Optional

These include all voluntary fasts. It should be borne in mind that the Prophet (peace be on him) asked Muslims not to fast for long periods, saying "You have duties to fulfill even with regard to yourself."

D. Forbidden

Prophet Muhammad (peace be on him) forbade fasting on the two *Eids, Eid-ul-Fitr* (the Festival of Fast Breaking) and *Eid-ul-*

Adha (the Festival of Sacrifice), and on the three days following *Eid-ul-Adha.* All these are days of thanksgiving, joy and happiness, while fasting involves hardship.

KEEPING THE FAST

The period of keeping fast is from before dawn (about two hours before sunrise) until sunset. During this period, one may not eat, drink or smoke, and married people in addition may not have marital relations. In addition, chewing or swallowing anything external or taking medicine through the mouth or nose is not permitted.

Eating, drinking or putting something in the mouth *unintentionally* (i.e., forgetting that you are fasting), use of perfume, ointments or skin creams, external medications, brushing the teeth or rinsing the mouth, swallowing saliva, washing one's body, does not break the fast.

However, eating, drinking, smoking or breaking the fast in any other manner *deliberately, without valid reason* (i.e., sickness, travel or the onset of menstruation), is an act of breaking one's commitment or intention to fast on a particular day (see below), and it carries a heavy penalty: either to feed sixty people the equivalent of one meal each, or to give the equivalent amount to sixty people in charity, or to fast for sixty days to make up for that one day's broken fast. On the other hand, if one does not wish to fast on a given day during Ramadan, whatever be the reasons, this is to be made up later, a day for a day.

EVENING MEAL

It is customary to break one's fast as soon as the sun has set with a light snack (often with one or three dates, according to the Prophet's custom). Before one begins to eat, he says, again according to the practice of the Prophet (peace be on him):

> O God, I have fasted for You, and I have believed in You, and with Your food I break the fast. In the name of God, the Merciful, the Mercy-giving.

This breaking of the fast is called *iftar.* It is followed by *Maghrib* (sunset) prayer, which may be followed at one's convenience by a full dinner. It is suggested not to overeat in order to compensate for the period of fasting. This is a good time to drink plenty of water or other fluid, which the body needs.

MORNING MEAL

It is also customary to take another meal during the night, as always beginning with the name of God *("Bismillah ar-Rahman ar-Raheem"),* resuming the fast at least twenty minutes before dawn begins to break. This meal is called *suhoor.* Any food will be found suitable for this meal, but common sense dictates that highly salted or highly seasoned food should not be taken and that protein foods are helpful in maintaining a high energy level during the day. After the pre-dawn meal is finished, one privately makes the intention of fasting for the day ahead. For example, one may say: "O God, I intend to fast today in obedience to Your command and only to seek Your pleasure." If one wishes, he may spend the interval between the end of eating until dawn in reading Qur'an or any other Islamic reading and as soon as dawn has broken, *Fajr* (dawn) prayer is performed.

EXEMPTIONS FROM FASTING

The following people are exempt from fasting:

A. Sick people whose health is likely to be severely affected by the observance of fasting. They may postpone the fast as long as they are sick and make up for it later, a day for a day.

B. People who are travelling (i.e., they have left their homes and are on the road, or when reaching their destination they have the intention of returning in a few days). Such people may not fast temporarily during their travel days only. They are to make up later the days which were missed, a day for a day. But it is better for them, as Qur'an points out, to observe the fast during their travels if they can do so without extraordinary hardship.

C. Pregnant women and nursing mothers may also not keep the fast, but they must make up for it later, a day for a day.

D. Women during the period of menstruation (maximum of ten days) or of confinement after childbirth (maximum of forty days) should not fast. They must postpone the fast until these periods are over and then make up for it, a day for a day.

E. Men and women who are too old and feeble to undertake the obligation and to bear its hardships. Such people are exempt from this duty, but if they can afford it, they must offer to at least one needy Muslim an average full meal (or its value) for each day of Ramadan on which they have not fasted. Whenever they are able to fast, even if it is for only one day of the month, they should do so and should compensate for the remainder.

F. Children under the age of puberty are exempt from the obligation of fasting. However, before they reach the age at which fasting becomes an obligation, it is good to encourage them to fast for a few days during Ramadan.

G. Insane persons are exempt from the obligation of fasting.

TARAWIH PRAYERS

These are supererogatory (additional, optional) prayers performed during the month of Ramadan after the fifth prayer of the day, 'Isha (night) prayer. These prayers consist of eight, ten or twenty units (rakat), each two or four units completing one cycle of the prayers. These prayers are not obligatory but are highly recommended, according to the Prophet's own practice (sunnah), especially during the last ten days of Ramadan.

ZAKAT-UL-FITR OR SADAQAT-UL-FITR

It is the religious duty of all Muslims to see that the poor in the community are not left uncared for. With this in view, Islam requires that all persons who can afford it should give a contribution to the poor any time before Eid day or on Eid day before the Eid prayer begins. This charity is known as zakat-ul-fitr or sadaqat-ul-fitr. The Holy Prophet (peace be on him) is reported to have said: "Fasting during Ramadan is not acceptable to God without sadaqat-ul-fitr" and "Sadaqat-ul-fitr is a means of purification of one who is fasting." This amount should be equivalent to at least one meal.

RECOMMENDATIONS DURING RAMADAN

Since Ramadan is a month of spiritual discipline, it is recommended that one should go beyond the regular prayers and fasting. Besides *Tarawih* prayers, other things are recommended.

A. One should try to complete the reading of Qur'an from beginning to end at least once during Ramadan. Needless to say, prayers should be observed with absolute regularity.

B. One of the functions of fasting is to make Muslims realize how it feels to be hungry, i.e., needy. Giving charity is therefore quite closely related to fasting and it should be given to the fullest extent one can afford.

C. *Zakat* is the Fourth Pillar of Islam. It is recommended that one should pay his annual *zakat* every Ramadan.

D. Restraining the temper, refraining from gossip and back-biting, and the doing of whatever is good and desirable at all times, but especially during Ramadan. Fasting and becoming angry or speaking ill of others do not go hand-in-hand.

EID-UL-FITR

After Ramadan, the month of fasting, has ended, *Eid-ul-Fitr*— the Festival of Fast Breaking—takes place on the first day of the succeeding month, Shawwal. *Eid* is a day of thanksgiving and rejoicing for the fulfillment of the obligation of fasting according to God's command. In the morning, at some time after sunrise and before midday, a special congregational prayer consisting of two units *(rakat),* with six to sixteen additional *takbirs* (recitations of *"Allahu Akbar"* [God is Most Great]), is offered, followed by a sermon *(khutba)* by the leader of the prayer (the *imam*). A period of marked joy and happiness follows the prayers. The Holy Prophet (peace be on him) has said: "A fasting person will have joy and happiness twice: when he breaks the fast [i.e., he will be full of joy because of breaking the fast], and when he meets his Lord on the Day of Judgment [he will be full of joy because he had kept his obligation of fasting]."

Muslims in Cameroon celebrate the end of Ramadan.

READING 10
Poor-due*

THE MEANING OF ZAKAT AND ITS IMPORTANCE

Zakat is the Fourth Pillar of Islam. It is an obligation *(fard),* prescribed by God on those Muslim men and women who possess enough means, to distribute a certain percentage of their annual savings or capital in goods or money among the poor and the needy. *Zakat* is assessed at the end of the year on both capital and savings from income. The details of percentages and the method of distribution and collection are based on the practices of Prophet Muhammad (peace be on him) and his Companions, and will be discussed in a later section of this unit.

The literal meaning of the word *zakat* is 'purity.' The Prophet (peace be on him) has said: "God has made *zakat* obligatory simply to purify your remaining property." There is no equivalent practice in other religions. Hence, while terms such as 'charity,' 'poor-tax,' 'alms-tax' and 'poor-due' have been coined by various translators, none of these terms actually conveys the true sense of the word *zakat. Zakat* is not a tax levied by a government, nor is it a voluntary contribution. It is first and foremost a duty enjoined by God and hence a form of worship. In Qur'an the payment of *zakat* is frequently mentioned in the same sentence or verse as the establishment of *salat* (prayers).

*Adapted from Islamic Correspondence Course, Unit 5B (Plainfield, Ind.: The Muslim Students' Association of the United States and Canada, 1974).

> Lo! Those who believe and do good deeds and establish *salat* and pay *zakat,* their reward is with their Sustainer; and no fear shall come upon them, nor shall they grieve. (2:277)

> These are verses of the Book full of wisdom, a guide and mercy to the doers of good—those who establish *salat* and pay *zakat* and have the assurance of the Hereafter. These are on guidance from their Sustainer, and these are the ones who will prosper. (31:1–5)

Thus, while *salat* is an act of worship through words and bodily action, *zakat* is a devotional act through one's wealth. Without the spirit of submission to God and love of Him, both acts are without spiritual and moral significance.

From a practical point of view, it is the duty of an Islamic state to collect *zakat* from every Muslim who meets the requirements for paying it. The first Caliph, Abu Bakr Siddiq, declared war on those tribes which refused to pay *zakat* while still professing Islam and observing daily prayers. He reasoned that the Divine law *(Shari'ah)* cannot be divided and that one cannot follow part of the Holy Book and cast aside other parts. However, in a non-Islamic state it is up to the individual Muslim to be conscientious enough to voluntarily fulfill this duty to God and to his community, and it is up to his brother Muslims to remind him of this duty.

THE SPIRIT OF ZAKAT

In the Holy Qur'an, wealth is referred to as God's bounty. God, as the Creator and Sustainer of the universe, is also the Owner of all things, including all the things which man possesses and uses.

> Who has created the heavens and the earth and sends down rain for you from the sky? With it We caused to grow orchards full of loveliness; it is not in your power to make trees grow in them. (27:60)

Since God is the true Owner of all things and we are merely His trustees, wealth is to be produced, distributed, acquired and spent in a way which is pleasing to Him. The acquisition of wealth is not an end in itself, nor is wealth to be squandered for meaningless or wasteful purposes, and above all it is not to be used in order to gain power over other people through exploitation or control of the means of livelihood. Qur'an and *Hadith* make it very clear that any form of gain which results in some injustice or harm to others is an act of disobedience to God. On the other hand,

Qur'an tells us that next to purity of faith, the most pleasing thing in the sight of God is kindness and charity, forbearance and forgiveness, and doing good to others.

> Those who spend in charity, whether in prosperity or adversity, who restrain anger and pardon people; for God loves those who do good to others. (3:134)

Thus, God enjoins on us humility before the Creator and His creatures, moderation in the satisfaction of our legitimate needs and desires, control of our appetites, and a spirit of generosity and charity, while He asks us to shun pride in ourselves and contempt for others, self-indulgence and pleasure-seeking, and greed for material things and worldly power. We find, therefore, that prayers *(salat)* are made obligatory to purify our hearts from every kind of pride, fasting *(siyam)* to control our appetites, and *zakat* to overcome greed. The spirit behind all these acts of worship ought to be the spirit of submission to God, gratitude for all His bounties, and hope for His forgiveness and mercy.

In particular, it is with gratitude and joy that a Muslim who possesses enough means that *zakat* is obligatory for him should fulfill his obligation—gratitude for the bounties which God has showered upon him and joy in being able to help others. Because the payment of *zakat* is a duty to God, no one should ever think of it as a favor done to the person who receives it. In fact, it is his right to receive it and the obligation of the giver to give it. Like any other act of worship in Islam, in giving *zakat* it is necessary that the intention of the giver and receiver be pure and honest.

THE BENEFITS OF ZAKAT

The moral and material benefits of *zakat* are obvious. Giving *zakat* purifies the heart of the giver from selfishness and greed for wealth and develops in him sympathy for the poor and needy. And receiving *zakat* purifies the heart of the recipient from envy and hatred of the rich and prosperous, and fosters in him a sense of good will toward his brother Muslims who, although they are better off, have shared their wealth with him for the sake of God.

God says in Qur'an:

To Him belong the keys of the heavens and earth; He enlarges or restricts the sustenance to whom He wills, for He knows full well all things. (42:12)

He has raised some of you in ranks above others that He may try you in the gifts He has given you. (6:165)

Thus, a Muslim, whether prosperous or needy, considers his condition in this world as a test from God. Those who have wealth have the obligation to be generous and charitable and to share the bounties of God with their brothers, while those who are poor have the obligation to be patient, to work to improve their situation, and to be free of envy. Qur'an tells us that it is not a man's wealth or position but his God-consciousness, the quality of his character, and the manner in which he uses whatever is given to him by God which determines his ultimate destiny in the Hereafter. The Prophet (peace be on him) has said: "The generous man is near God, near Paradise, near men, and far from Hell, but the miserly man is far from God, far from Paradise, far from men, and near Hell. Indeed, an ignorant man who is generous is dearer to God than a worshipper who is miserly."

The economic objective of Islam is just and humane distribution of wealth, as stated in Qur'an:

. . . so that this (wealth) may not circulate solely among the rich from among you. (59:7)

Thus, Islam neither approves of hoarding and unlimited building up of capital, nor of compulsory equal distribution of wealth, as both are unjust. Its teaching encourages the earning of a livelihood and acquisition of wealth by lawful, honest and productive means, and enjoins the just sharing of the acquired wealth among the workers, the investors and the community at large. The community's share in the produced wealth is zakat and sadaqah (charity), the first an obligatory and the second a voluntary contribution from individuals. Zakat, when honestly practiced, results in freeing the society from class distinctions, rivalries, suspicion and corruption. It produces a community of people who love and respect each other, and who have sympathy and concern for each other's welfare.

Giving zakat is not a matter of pride. It is a devotional act, like salat, on the completion of which the contributor should be thankful to God for the fulfillment of his obligation and pray for the forgiveness of his sins.

KINDS OF PROPERTY ON WHICH ZAKAT IS OBLIGATORY

Zakat is compulsory on cash, cattle and crops (three c's). The regulations differ for each of these categories. As the detailed system of computation in the last two categories is rather complicated, it will not be discussed here. Such information is available in standard books on Islamic jurisprudence.

For cash, the minimum rate is two and one-half percent (2½%). *Zakat* should be given only on the net balance after all lawful expenses have been met at the end of the year. The rate mentioned above is only a lower limit. There is no upper limit, except that one should not deprive himself and his dependents from meeting their lawful necessities. Beyond these obligations, the more one gives, the greater the benefit on both the giver and the recipient.

RECIPIENTS OF ZAKAT

Those who are eligible to receive *zakat* are mentioned in the Holy Qur'an.

The alms are only for the poor, the needy, those who collect them, those whose hearts are to be reconciled, to free the captives and the debtors, for the cause of God, and for the travellers; a duty imposed by God. God is All-Knowing, All-Wise. (9:60)

It should be remembered that these categories of persons who are to be helped by *zakat* were laid down fourteen hundred years ago. They are equally applicable to our own time.

1. **The poor:** Those who are unable to work or do not have sufficient means to support themselves and their families, or those who are engaged in the way of God and are unable to earn their livelihood. Those who do not ask are preferable.

2. **The needy:** Those people who, due to some calamity, have lost their possessions should be supported by these funds in order to provide them means for earning a living.

3. **Zakat collectors:** The salaries of these workers may be paid from this fund. According to some authorities, this category refers to the revenue department or even the entire government of an Islamic state or to workers in a public fund.

4. **Converts:** Those people who have embraced Islam and consequently lost all their worldly assets should be helped, and attempts should be made to settle them in a normal life.

A seller of fruit in the market of Jiddah, Saudi Arabia. Crops are among the kinds of property on which zakat *is imposed.*

5. **People who are not free:** This category would include payment of ransom for freeing Muslim hostages or prisoners of war from their captors.

6. **Debtors:** People who are unable to pay debts incurred due to pressing lawful needs. Those who have incurred debts by extravagance in marriage and other purposes of display of wealth and ostentation cannot claim help from these funds.

7. **Wayfarers and travellers:** Those people who are rendered helpless in a foreign country due to lawful reasons such as preaching Islam, pursuing an education, business, etc., may be helped under this heading. The money may also be given to welfare organizations which dispense help of this kind.

8. **In the way of God:** This category embraces general help to the public or to a good cause for which people are striving. Under this heading, money could be utilized as follows:

A. It could be given to those who can help propagate the message of Islam;

B. It could be provided as stipends to students, scholars and researchers;

C. It could be used in organizing or improving organizations beneficial to the community, for example, hospitals, educational institutions, libraries, mosques, groups working for the service of Islam, and for the propagation of knowledge.

SOME REGULATIONS CONCERNING ZAKAT

The legal dependents of the contributor may not receive *zakat* from him.

Money exceeding the recipient's requirements is not to be given, nor may the recipient accept more than enough to meet his requirements.

Taxes which are paid to the government are not included in the category of *zakat*.

The contributor should not indulge in pride nor seek fame by carrying out this duty, but if the mention of his name is likely to encourage others to pay *zakat*, it is permissible to give his name.

It is not necessary to tell the recipient that he is receiving *zakat* money. If there are deserving persons who will not accept the money if they know it is *zakat*, it can be given without specifying its source. The contributor, however, still gives it as his *zakat* payment.

Zakat may be distributed directly to the individuals or organizations mentioned above. The contributor should use his best possible judgment to find the most deserving beneficiaries. In the past, when there were legally constituted Islamic governments, *zakat* was collected through official channels and its distribution was the function of a special department of the government. In the present day, however, especially in non-Muslim countries, giving *zakat* is an obligation for which each Muslim adult must take responsibility each year himself. In North America, Muslims may give their *zakat* directly to some deserving needy person, of whom there are many in every community, or he may give it for use as *zakat* to some Islamic organization, such as the Muslim Students' Association of United States and Canada, which has a *zakat* fund. Possible suggested uses of the collected *zakat* money on this continent would be in helping our brother Muslims in other countries, in organizing youth camps and training centers for the education of Muslim children growing up here, in helping organizations serving Islam in the United States and Canada, in supporting Muslim educational institutions or hospitals, and in any other efforts for the cause of Islam.

SADAQAH (CHARITY)

Zakat is an obligation on Muslim men and women who are better off financially. *Sadaqah* (charity) refers to any other act of charity.

1. **Charity—an essential part of righteousness:** To give to help others from one's possessions, no matter whether they are many or few, is a necessary part of a Muslim's sense of submission to God and his concern for his fellow human beings. God says in Qur'an:

> You shall not attain righteousness unless you spend on others of that which you love, and whatever you spend, verily God has knowledge of it. (3:92)

The Holy Prophet (peace be on him) has said: "Sons of Adam! To give away what is beyond your needs is better for you and to withhold it is worse for you, but you are not blamed for having sufficiency. Give first to those who are dependent on you."

2. **What to spend in charity:** God says in Qur'an:

> They ask thee what to spend (in charity). Say: What is beyond your needs. (2:219)

O you who believe! Spend of the good things which you have earned, and of that which We bring forth from the earth for you, and do not seek to give the bad things (in charity), when you would not take them for yourselves except with disdain. (2:267)

The Prophet (peace be on him) exhorted: "Spend; do not calculate and so have God calculating against you; do not hoard and so have God hoarding from you; but give such small amounts as you can."

3. **How to give charity:** The best charity is that which is given in secret, in order to respect the dignity of the recipient and to keep the motives of the giver free of pride or desire for praise. Qur'an says:

O you who believe! Do not cancel your charity by reminders of your generosity or by injury, like those who spend their substance to be seen men but do not believe either in God or in the Last Day. (2:264)

Kind words and the covering of faults are better than charity followed by injury. God is free of all wants, and He is most forbearing. (2:263)

The Prophet (peace be on him) has said: "The best charity is that which the right hand gives and the left hand does not know of it."

4. **Recipients of charity:** Charity starts with one's own family and dependents and extends to relatives, to the poor and the needy of the community, to widows and orphans, debtors, travellers, those who strive or who migrate in the cause of God, and finally to any others in need. Qur'an says:

They ask thee what they should spend (in charity). Say: Whatever of your wealth you spend shall be for the parents and for the near of kin and the orphans and the needy and the traveller; and whatever good you do, verily, God has full knowledge of it. (2:215; also 9:60)

(Charity is) for those in need, who, in God's cause are restricted (from travel) and cannot move about in the land, seeking (for trade or work). The ignorant man thinks, because of their dignity, that they are free from want. You shall know them by their mark: they do not beg insistently from all and sundry. And whatever of good you give, be assured God knows it well. (2:273)

Finally, in a broader sense, it is important to stress that the meaning of charity is not confined to money or things given to help someone in need. It includes everything we do or say to help

A research technician at King Faisal Hospital in Saudi Arabia. Hospitals, as recipients of zakat, fall in category 8: "In the way of God."

others—our time, our energy, our concern, our sympathy, our attitude of support, our words of kindness, our prayers. To care for the needs of a neighbor, to minister to the wants of a child, to visit the sick, to go to the funeral of an acquaintance, to console the bereaved—all these are acts of charity. There are many *hadiths* (saying of the Prophet) which emphasize clearly how broad the meaning of charity is, among which are the following: "When you smile in your brother's face, or enjoin what is reputable, or forbid what is objectionable, or direct someone who has lost his way, or help a man who has bad eyesight, or remove stones, thorns and bones from the road, or pour water from your bucket into your brother's, it counts to you as charity," and "Every act of kindness is charity." May God Most High guide each of us to do our utmost, in the true Islamic spirit of brotherhood, in charity.

READING 11
Pilgrimage*

THE MEANING OF HAJJ

The Arabic word *hajj* means "to set out for a definite purpose."
Specifically, it refers to the pilgrimage to Ka'bah, which is situated
in the city of Mecca in Saudi Arabia, and the performance of
certain observances *(manasik)* during the months prescribed for
hajj. The observances of *hajj* are based on Qur'an (2:196–203,
5:98–100, 22:27–32) and *Sunnah* (the practice of Prophet
Muhammad, peace be on him), and they commemorate certain
events in the lives of the Prophet Abraham, his wife Hagar, and
their son the Prophet Ishmael (peace be on them). These observances and their significance will be described later. Here we
would like to stress the fact that the main object of *hajj*, as of any
other form of Islamic worship, is to create the spirit of submission to God and to nourish spiritual joy. The Holy Prophet has
said:

> Those who perform the *hajj* or *'umra* are people who have come to
> visit God [that is, they have come with the sole intention of
> worshipping God]. If they supplicate Him, He will respond to them,
> and if they ask of Him forgiveness, He will forgive them.

*Adapted from Islamic Correspondence Course, Unit 5A (Plainfield, Ind.: The Muslim
Students' Association of the United States and Canada, 1974).

THE SIGNIFICANCE OF HAJJ

The spirit of *hajj* is the spirit of total sacrifice—of personal comforts, worldly pleasures, the acquisition of wealth, the companionship of relatives and friends, vanities of dress and personal appearance, pride relating to birth, national origin, accomplishments, work or social status. This sacrifice of self was attained to the highest degree by the Prophet Abraham (peace be on him), who is known as 'The Friend of God' *(Khalil-ul-Allah)*. The story of his sacrifice is narrated in Qur'an:

> [Abraham said] "O my Sustainer! Grant me a righteous (son)!" So We gave him the good news of a boy [Ishmael] ready to suffer and forbear. Then, when (the son) reached (the age of serious) work with him, he said, "O my son! I see in vision that I offer you in sacrifice: now see what is your view." (The son) said: "O my father! Do as you are commanded. You will find me, if God so wills, one practicing patience and constancy." So when they had submitted their wills (to God), and he [Abraham] had laid him [Ishmael] prostrate on his forehead (for sacrifice), We called out to him, "O Abraham! You have already fulfilled the vision!"—thus indeed do We reward those who do right. For this was obviously a trial. And We ransomed him with a great sacrifice. And We left (this blessing) for him among generations (to come) in later times: "Peace and salutation to Abraham!" (37:100–109)

Although the events to which this narrative refers occurred many centuries ago (roughly 2000 B.C.), they have a very clear and direct meaning for us today, as they did at the time of Prophet Muhammad (peace be on him). The significance of Abraham's willingness to sacrifice his son, who was dearer to him than anything else in the world, at God's command, is a clear demonstration that to him obedience to God was more important than any earthly possession or tie, no matter how precious it might be. The spirit of submission to God cannot be illustrated for us in any clearer manner than this.

The *hajj* also signifies the brotherhood of all Muslims, which is demonstrated and emphasized in a concrete manner in this greatest of all international assemblies. If the true spirit of *hajj* were carried through into our daily lives, Muslims everywhere could achieve the same oneness and the same unity now known only during *hajj*, for at that time the ordinary distinctions and differences among human beings are erased. During *hajj*

Muslims of every race and color and language, of diverse cultures and backgrounds, of various social, economic and educational levels, all respond to the call of God, all dressed in the same simple manner—the two pieces of white, unsewn cloth which constitute the pilgrim's dress—all performing the same actions in the same way for the same single purpose: the glorification of Almighty God. This oneness of physical appearance and singleness of purpose also impresses upon the minds of the pilgrims that all human beings are equal in the sight of God and that all will be accountable to Him. Thus *hajj* also reminds Muslims of the ultimate assembly of the Day of Judgment, when all human beings will stand equal before Almighty God, to receive their reward or punishment.

Hajj also reminds Muslims of the birth, rise and expansion of Islam, the overthrow of idolatry, the establishment of the worship of One God, and the difficulties and achievements of the Holy Prophet Muhammad (peace be on him) and the early Muslims.

MECCA

Mecca is the sacred city of Islam, located in the Arabian peninsula. The city lies in a long, irregular valley fringed with low hills and exposed passes. Its climate is extremely hot and dry. Despite its heat and sterility, which make it poorly suited for human habitation, Mecca was in times past the trade and cultural center of Arabia. The historical importance of Mecca is related to Ka'bah, the Prophet Abraham, his son the Prophet Ishmael (peace be on them), and their descendants.

Mecca and Medina (situated some 225 miles northwest of Mecca) are the two cities most dear to Muslims because of their great reverence and love for the Holy Prophet Muhammad (peace be on him). The Prophet was born in Mecca and was buried in Medina, and, excepting short periods of travel, spent all his life in these two cities.

KA'BAH

The word Ka'bah means 'a cube-shaped structure.' It refers in particular to the cube-shaped building in Mecca constructed of stone and mortar, measuring approximately 45 feet in height, 33

There is nothing inside the Ka'aba now except the three pillars which support the roof and gold and silver lamps suspended from the ceiling.

feet in width and 50 feet in length, which is generally covered with a black cloth decorated with Qur'anic verses worked in gold. Ka'bah is also known as the Most Ancient House, the Sacred Mosque, and the House of God. Muslims all over the world face the direction of Ka'bah when they perform their five daily prayers in accordance with the injunction:

> Turn then thy face in the direction of the Sacred Mosque. Wherever you are, turn your faces in that direction [for prayers]. (2:144)

The direction from any place on the globe toward Ka'bah is known as *qibla*.

Ka'bah was the first structure built by man consecrated to the worship of One God. It was erected in antiquity by the Prophet Abraham and his son Ishmael (peace be on them). Qur'an refers to the building of Ka'bah in several verses:

> And when We assigned to Abraham the site of the House. . . . (22:26)—And when Abraham and Ishmael were raising the foundations of the House (they prayed): "Our Sustainer! Accept Thou this from us. Surely Thou art All-Hearing, All-Knowing. . . ." (2:127)—And We commanded Abraham and Ishmael: "Purify My House for those who visit it and those who meditate therein, and those who bow down and prostrate." (2:125)—And call to mind the occasion when Abraham said: "My Sustainer! Make this city secure and save me and my descendants from worshipping idols." (14:35)

However, in the course of time, the belief in the Oneness of God, the concept of submission to him, the significance of the Ka'bah and the spiritual aspect of *hajj* faded out of people's minds. They reverted to idol worship and superstitious pagan customs. Before the coming of Prophet Muhammad (peace be on him), there were 360 idols in Ka'bah and pilgrimage to it had degenerated into a mere funfair. When the Meccans submitted to Islam in 8 A.H. (After *Hijra*), the Prophet cleared Ka'bah of all the idols and revived the true spirit of *hajj* according to God's command.

It should be stressed that Ka'bah is not the birthplace of Prophet Muhammad and that pilgrimage to Ka'bah does not in any way signify the worship of the Prophet (peace be on him) or any other human being, as pilgrimage does in some religions. We venerate Ka'bah and the other holy places for their history and associations, but *not* for themselves. This cannot be emphasized too strongly, for God Most High alone is the object of our worship, in *hajj* as in any other form of Islamic worship.

HAJJ—AN OBLIGATION (FARD)

Hajj is the Fifth Pillar of Islam. It is obligatory *(fard)* at least once in a lifetime for any Muslim man or woman who fulfills the following conditions: at the time he (or she) intends to perform *hajj*, he should be sane, in sound health, free from debts, and should have enough resources not only to defray his own travel expenses but also to take care of his dependents who have remained at home. It is a further condition that peace and security for his life and property exist on the way to Mecca and back. God says in Qur'an:

> And pilgrimage to the House [Ka'bah] is a duty people owe to God, for him who can afford the journey. (3:97)

If a Muslim dies without ever having performed *hajj*, any of his dependents or any other person whom they select can perform *hajj* on behalf of the deceased, if he fulfills the above requirements at the time of his death. A sick or disabled person who otherwise meets these requirements may choose another person to perform *hajj* on his behalf. At each stage of *hajj* the substitute person first performs the observances of *hajj* for himself and then again on behalf of the person whom he represents.

'UMRA (THE MINOR PILGRIMAGE), HAJJ (THE MAJOR PILGRIMAGE), AND HAJJU AT-TAMATTU' (THE INTERRUPTED PILGRIMAGE)

1. *'UMRA:* Any Muslim may visit Mecca at any time and perform *'umra,* the Minor Pilgrimage. This consists of putting on *ihram* (the pilgrim's dress) and performing *tawaf* and *sa'i* (see paragraphs 2 and 3 in the following section, "The Observances of Hajj"). The *ihram* is taken off after *sa'i. 'Umra* is complete in itself, and it is not a substitute for *hajj,* the Major Pilgrimage.

2. *HAJJ:* The observances of *hajj* are concentrated on 8th, 9th and 10th of Dhul-Hijja. They consist of putting on *ihram,* performing *tawaf* and *sa'i,* taking part in the observances of Arafat, Muzdalifa and Mina, and the sacrifice of *Eid-ul-Adha.*

On the basis of *sunnah* (the practice of the Prophet, peace be on him), it is the general practice to include *'umra* in performing *haji*. This is done simply by including *'umra* in the intention *(niyat)*.

3. *HAJJU AT-TAMATTU':* If one wishes, he may arrive in Mecca as early as the beginning of the month of Shawwal, perform *'umra*, put aside *ihram*, and then wait to perform *hajj* at the specified time in Dhul-Hijja. This is called *hajju at-tamattu'*, the Interrupted Pilgrimage.

The months of Shawwal, Dhul-Qu'da and the first twelve days of Dhul-Hijja (the tenth, eleventh and twelfth months of the Islamic calendar) are specified for *hajj*. This means that one could come to Mecca for *hajju at-tamattu'* at any time between the beginning of Shawwal and the days specified for *hajj*, while for *hajj* alone one would arrive in the early part of Dhul-Hijja. As the Islamic calendar is regulated by the lunar cycle, these months rotate through different seasons of the solar year.

THE OBSERVANCES OF HAJJ

The obligatory *(fard)* observances of *hajj*, together with their historical significance, will be described here briefly in the order in which they are performed.

1. *IHRAM,* the physical and spiritual state of consecration to God: Before approaching Mecca, the pilgrim takes a full bath if possible (or he may perform ablution—*wudu* or *tayammum*—if it is not possible), before putting on the garments of *ihram.* In *ihram* attire, he expresses his intention by saying:

> O God, I intend to perform *hajj*, and I am taking *ihram* for it. Make it easy for me, and accept it from me.

The putting on of *ihram* is followed by a two-*rakat* (two-unit) prayer *(salat)*.

The *ihram* dress, which all male pilgrims wear, consists of two sheets of ordinary unsewn white cloth, one covering the lower part of the body to the ankles and the other draped over one shoulder, covering the upper half of the body. While there is no

A pilgrim tent at Arafat.

specific *ihram* for women, they should put on clean, plain clothing at the time of entering *ihram,* wearing long-sleeved garments which reach to the ankles and covering their hair.

Ihram signifies a state of peace, self-denial and total submission to God. The putting on of the pilgrim's dress is symbolic of renouncing worldly and material goals and vanities. The pilgrim

Because of the great numbers of people, it is often late in the day when one finally performs tawaf.

who is in a state of consecration must abstain even from ordinarily lawful satisfactions and pleasures until the observances of *hajj* are over and *ihram* is put aside. In the state of *ihram*, he may not use any other form of dress, jewelry or personal adornments, perfume or scent, may not shave, trim his hair or nails, or engage in marital intercourse. During the days in *ihram* there may be no wrangling or argument, no rudeness, no discussion of the opposite sex, no uprooting of any growing thing, and no hunting. Bodily, the pilgrim is to be devoted to the acts of the pilgrimage; spiritually he or she is to be concerned with the worship of Almighty God, self-examination, an awareness of the meaning of his devotional acts and words, and a sense of the brotherhood and unity of all Muslims.

From the beginning of the observances until the first pillar is stoned at Mina, the pilgrim makes many devotional calls. These calls are said aloud, in unison with one's fellow pilgrims at each state of the observances.

2. *TAWAF* (going around): On entering the great courtyard which encircles Ka'bah, the pilgrim recites:

> O God, Thou are Peace, and peace comes from Thee, so, our Sustainer, give us peace and admit us to the Garden, the Abode of Peace [Paradise].

He then walks around Ka'bah seven times, starting his circuits from the corner of the Black Stone, a relic from the original structure of the Sacred Ka'bah built by Abraham, after kissing, touching or raising his hand toward the Black Stone, according to the practice *(sunnah)* of the Holy Prophet (peace be on him). During each of the seven circuits, different recitations are said, the pilgrims in groups repeating the prayers after the pilgrim guide who is the leader of their group. If one cannot follow the words of the guide, he may praise God in his own words.

3. *SA'I* (hastening): On completion of the circuits of Ka'bah, the pilgrim proceeds toward as-Safa and al-Marwa, two small hills situated nearby in the center of Mecca. Long ago, the Prophet Abraham, at the command of God, left his wife Hagar and his son Ishmael (peace be on them) here with a small supply of food and water, to live in the deserted land of Mecca. Their ration of food and water was soon gone. The scorching desert sun created an intense thirst in the unsheltered child and his mother. Hagar ran up and down as-Safa and al-Marwa to see if she could find water

for her distressed child. Meanwhile, the boy had dug his heels into the sand, and when Hagar returned to him, water was welling up from the floor of the desert at his feet. With the precious liquid she quenched the thirst of her son, who was near death. Because of this well, which continued to flow, a group of tribesmen settled in the valley of Mecca near Hagar and Ishmael. The spring, known as the Well of Zamzam, has been in existence ever since, although its location was later lost. It was eventually discovered again by Abdul Muttalib, the grandfather of Prophet Muhammad (peace be on him), when its location was shown to him by God in a dream. The Well of Zamzam is held in great reverence, and pilgrims drink from it during their pilgrimage.

God has prescribed the remembrance of Hagar's attempts to find water as an important part of the observances of *hajj*. Each pilgrim ascends as-Safa. At the top he makes devotional calls, descends from the hill, walks the distance to al-Marwa and climbs it.

4. *ARAFAT* and *MUZDALIFA:* After sunrise on 9th of Dhul-Hijja, the pilgrim sets out for Mount Arafat (about thirteen miles distant), either on foot or by conveyance, reciting *talbiya*. The valley of Arafat is a great barren plain large enough to contain the entire assembly of pilgrims, who in recent years have numbered several hundred thousand. Here, at high noon on 9th of Dhul-Hijja, all the pilgrims rise to their feet to worship their Lord, examine themselves, declare their repentance, and realize the true meaning of the brotherhood of all Muslims. Here *Zuhr* and *'Asr* prayers are performed in congregation. The Holy Prophet (peace be on him) has said concerning these prayers, "The best of prayers is the prayer of the day of Arafat." Just after sunset, all the pilgrims break camp and hurry to Muzdalifa, about five miles distant, where everyone performs *Maghrib* and *'Isha* prayers and passes the night.

5. *MINA:* On the morning of the 10th of Dhul-Hijja, the pilgrims return to Mina, a small village which was passed earlier on the way from Mecca to Arafat. In Mina there are three stone pillars representing three positions where the devil (Satan) tried to tempt Prophet Ishmael (peace be on him) to rebellion when his father was leading him to the place of sacrifice. Ishmael drove away the devil by throwing stones at him, and in Mina the pilgrims

throw stones which they have gathered at the three pillars to signify the rejection of evil promptings.

6. *EID-UL-ADHA* (The Feast of Sacrifice): After stoning the first of the three pillars, the pilgrims sacrifice a sheep, goat or camel, following the practice *(sunnah)* of the Prophet Abraham who sacrificed a ram when God spared him the sacrifice of his son Ishmael (peace be on them). While *Eid-ul-Adha* is actually a part of the observances of *hajj*, it is also celebrated throughout the Muslim world, and every Muslim who can afford it sacrifices an animal on this occasion. Part of the meat is distributed among the poor and needy for food, and the remainder is used to feed the household and shared with relatives and friends.

It should be pointed out that the word 'sacrifice' used in this context does not have the usual meaning of atonement for sin or an attempt to appease an angry deity. It signifies the remembrance of the willingness of Abraham (peace be on him) to sacrifice his own desires and attachments in submission to God, and it serves as a reminder to Muslims that they should be ready, if required, to sacrifice everything they have—even their lives—in the cause of God and his religion. God says in Qur'an:

> It is not their meat nor blood that reaches God. It is your piety that reaches Him. He has made them [animals] subject to you that you might glorify God for His guidance to you. And proclaim the good tidings to all who do right. (22:37)

After this, the pilgrims shave, slip or cut off a few strands of hair, which signifies the end of wearing *ihram* dress, although all the prohibitions of *ihram* apart from returning to ordinary dress are in effect until after the second circuiting of Ka'bah which is performed on 10th of Dhul-Hijja or the following day. Its completion releases the pilgrims from the prohibitions of *ihram*. The pilgrims remain in the valley of Mina for two or three days after 10th of Dhul-Hijja worshipping God, and additional stonings of the pillars take place during this time. Some pilgrims spend most of the day in Mecca, returning to Mina only at night; but all must remain in Mina for at least two nights following the night of the 10th. The observances of *hajj* are complete by 13th of Dhul-Hijja.

Most of the pilgrims visit Medina, where Prophet Muhammad's Tomb and Mosque are located. Some also visit the Farthest Mosque, built on the site of Solomon's Temple in Jerusalem, sacred to Muslims because of its connection with the Night of the

Journey and the Ascension. These visits, however, are not obligatory and are not part of the observances of *hajj*.

PRACTICAL SUGGESTIONS

The details of the observances of *hajj* and *'umra* are intricate
and lengthy, and may be found in any standard book on the
subject, such as "The Sacred Journey" by Ahmad Kamal, from
which most of the material in this unit is taken. Any Muslim
intending to go on *hajj* or *'umra* must obtain a valid visa from the
Saudi Arabia Embassy. One can obtain the service of a
professional guide, licensed by the Saudi government, who is
responsible for the material and spiritual welfare of the pilgrims
under his care and who acts as interpreter for pilgrims who do not
speak Arabic.

The normal population of Mina and Arafat is a few hundred persons. For one week every year the towns shelter over a
million pilgrims. Meccan merchants close their shops and take provisions to Mina and Arafat.

PART III
The Islamic Way of Life

Islam, by means of its belief system and its forms of worship, fosters certain qualities in its followers. These qualities are supported by the Islamic moral and ethical system. Muslims possessing these qualities and applying these moral precepts live together under the social system which Islam prescribes. They follow certain patterns in their day-to-day living. Part III presents a picture of Islam as a total way of life.

Moroccan merchant weighs potatoes in an open-air market.

READING 12
Moral Teachings of Islam*

THE OBJECTIVE OF ISLAMIC TEACHINGS: A BALANCED LIFE

Qur'an tells us that everyone is born with pure faith—*Iman.*

> So set thy direction to the pure faith, the pattern of God on which He has made mankind. (30:30)

That is to say, it is part of man's basic nature to believe in the Oneness of God and to be inclined toward good deeds. Qur'an also says:

> We indeed created man in the best of patterns. (95:4)

In this respect Islam's view of man contrasts with those religions which burden man's soul with "original sin" or consider man's physical needs and biological desires to be obstacles to his spiritual aspirations.

Islam takes an integrated and wholesome view of man, recognizing that his personality is indivisible. As a matter of emphasis or for the purpose of discussion, we may speak of the spiritual, intellectual, emotional, biological and other aspects of man's per-

*Adapted and abridged from Islamic Correspondence Course, Unit 8 (Plainfield, Ind.: The Muslim Students' Association of the United States and Canada, 1974).

sonality, but all these aspects are in fact inseparable from one another. Thus Islam does not recognize a division and a duality between religious and secular, between "sacred and profane," between spiritual and material, between what is done with the thought of God and what is done with God put out of one's mind. When Qur'an prescribes acts of worship—prayer, fasting, poor-due, pilgrimage—these acts contain and imply physical, emotional, intellectual, social and material benefits for Muslims. When it sets forth some injunction concerning practical matters—for example, business transactions, administration of justice, the practice of usury, marriage and divorce, eating and drinking, and so on—it does not neglect the spiritual aspect of man.

A truly balanced and God-conscious life, then, is an equilibrium of the various aspects of human existence, not stifling one part and placing too much emphasis on the other. Praying, fasting, reading Qur'an and other devotional acts are very basic and essential aspects of a Muslim's life, but they must go hand-in-hand with other basic and essential aspects of his life, all being done with the same spirit of God-consciousness and striving to please Him. A Muslim is not asked nor expected to destroy his natural desires and inclinations, but to make every aspect of himself Muslim, disciplining his desires and inclinations to come within the limits set by God.

An Iranian religious instruction class.

Since in Islam there are no specifically "sacred" acts, no sacraments or rites requiring a special class of ordained individuals to perform them, Islam does not have, nor does it require, any priestly class to administer the spiritual affairs of Muslims. All human affairs are considered to be the joint responsibility of all the people, while each individual is responsible for seeing that he personally does not transgress the limits prescribed by God. Qur'an exhorts:

> Let there arise out of you a group of people inviting to all that is good, enjoining what is right and forbidding what is wrong: they are the successful. (3:104)

The practical significance of this injunction is that each Muslim should strive to learn what God has enjoined and forbidden, to act upon it, to teach it to others, and to establish God's laws on earth.

THE INFINITE WISDOM OF THE DIVINE LAWS

As Muslims, we realize that God's injunctions are not arbitrary, whimsical, despotic or impossible to act upon. On the contrary, God in His infinite wisdom and mercy has outlined certain moral laws in order to meet the needs of man, physical as well as spiritual. These laws are constant and immutable, just as are the "natural laws" of God which govern the rest of His creation. Because the total nature of man is known only to his Creator, these laws are timeless and universal, taking into consideration all aspects of man's condition, avoiding extremes and outlining a middle path.

Let us now see what some of the moral teachings of Islam are in regard to the various aspects of man's life—that is, his personal character, interpersonal relationships, social responsibilities, economic and administrative affairs, and his striving in the cause of God.

PERSONAL CHARACTER

Since the quality of a society depends upon the quality of the individuals who are its members, we will discuss personal character first.

Among the teachings of Islam, great emphasis is laid on God-consciousness, which is an approximate translation of the word *taqwa. Taqwa* refers to an attitude of mind, the awareness of God and consciousness of one's responsibility to Him. As such, it is mentioned in Qur'an as being the foundation of a Muslim's character.

> The most honorable among you in the sight of God is the one who is most God-conscious. (49:13)

God-consciousness provides man with a sound conscience.

> O you who believe! If you remain conscious of God, He will grant you a criterion (to judge between right and wrong). . . . (8:29)

> The Prophet (peace be on him) has said: If, through fear of God, tears—even a small drop—fall from any believer's eyes, he will be kept away from Hell by God.

This *hadith* clarifies how unmistakably the conduct of man is governed by his awareness of his responsibility to God, and how even a small element of this awareness in a man's heart can make the greatest difference in his life, both here and Hereafter.

In the teachings of Islam, great emphasis is placed on humility, modesty, control of passions and desires, truthfulness, integrity, patience and steadfastness. We are enjoined to fulfill all our promises and contracts, to keep all trusts, to meet our engagements, and to repay our debts.

> For in God's sight are all His servants— . . . those who are patient, truthful, devout, who spend in charity, and who pray for forgiveness at daybreak. (3:15, 17)

> And vie with one another to attain to your Sustainer's forgiveness and to a Paradise as vast as the heavens and the earth, which awaits the God-conscious, who spend for charity in time of plenty and in time of hardship, and restrain their anger, and pardon their fellow men, for God loves those who do good; who, when they have committed a shameful deed or have (otherwise) sinned against themselves, remember God and ask for forgiveness for their sins— for who but God could forgive sins?—and do not persist knowingly in doing whatever (wrong) they did. These it is who shall have as their reward forgiveness from their Sustainer, and gardens through which running waters flow, therein to abide: how excellent a reward for those who labor! (3:133-136)

> Establish regular prayer, enjoin what is just, and forbid what is wrong; and bear patiently whatever may befall you; for this is true constancy. And do not swell your cheek (with pride) at men, nor walk in insolence through the earth, for God does not love any man proud and boastful. And be moderate in your pace and lower your voice; for the harshest of sounds, indeed, is the braying of the ass. (31:18–19)

> And do not cover truth with falsehood, nor conceal the truth when you know (what it is). (2:42)

God has forbidden certain things which are indecent or harmful. It is our responsibility to abstain from them, and we should in fact try to avoid situations which lead to temptation.

> Do not come near to illicit sexual relations; surely it is an indecency and an evil way. (17:32)

> Let those who do not find the means for marriage keep themselves chaste, until God gives them the means out of His grace. (24:33)

> O you who believe! Intoxicants and games of chance [gambling] and idolatrous practices and the divining of the future are but a loathsome evil of Satan's doing: shun it, then, so that you might be

graced with good everlasting. By means of intoxicants and games of chance Satan seeks only to sow enmity and hatred among you and to turn you away from the remembrance of God and from prayer. Will you not then desist? (5:93-94)

In a way which summarizes the moral character of a Muslim, the Prophet (peace be on him) said:

> My Sustainer has given me nine commands: to remain conscious of God, whether in private or in public; to speak justly, whether angry or pleased; to show moderation both when poor and when rich; to reunite friendship with those who have broken it off with me; to give to him who refuses me; to forgive him who has wronged me; that my silence should be occupied with thought; that my looking should be an admonition; and that I should command what is right.

INTERPERSONAL RELATIONSHIPS

If one were to summarize by one word the Islamic teaching regarding interpersonal relationships, it would be with the single Arabic word *hilm*, which in English means "forbearance, kindness and forgiveness." Since all people have limitations and weaknesses and make errors of judgment, it is arrogant and presumptuous on anyone's part to pass judgments on others, to be intolerant, to treat people with contempt, or to mock or humiliate anyone.

> . . . [Those who] restrain their anger, and pardon their fellow men, for God loves those who do good. . . . (3:134)
>
> Kind words and the covering of faults are better than charity followed by injury. (2:263)
>
> The Prophet (peace be on him), on being asked how many times one ought to forgive his servant's mistakes, said: "Seventy times a day." Then he added: "If you cannot bear your servant's weaknesses, release him from your service."

It is part of forbearance and kindness to refrain from gossip, from prying into the affairs of others, and from saying anything behind a person's back which he would not like to have said about himself. We are not to discuss the affairs of other people secretly except when it is with a view of doing them some good. The faults of others, if known to us, should be concealed rather than exposed. We are not to shame others, as it generates a response of defiance and guilt rather than the real awareness of error. We are to refrain from passing judgments on the quality of others' faith and sincerity. We are enjoined not to talk about evil deeds or happenings except in cases where some social action is required; and we should remove ourselves from any conversation in which things are discussed which are filthy, degrading or make a joke of religion.

> In most of their secret talks there is no good: but if one exhorts to a deed of charity or justice or conciliation between men, (secrecy is permissible): to him who does this, seeking the good pleasure of God, We shall soon give a reward of highest value. (4:114)

> God does not love that evil should be openly mentioned, unless it be by him who has been wronged (thereby). (4:148)

> O you who believe! If a wicked person comes to you with any news, ascertain the truth, lest you harm people unwittingly, and afterwards become full of repentance for what you have done. (49:6)

> The Prophet (peace be on him) has said: The proof of a Muslim's sincerity is that he pays no heed to that which is not his business.

> The Prophet has also said: The Muslim is he from whose tongue and hand the Muslims are safe.

SOCIAL RESPONSIBILITIES

The teachings of Islam concerning social responsibilities are based on kindness and consideration of others. Since a broad injunction to be kind is likely to be ignored in specific situations, Islam lays emphasis on specific acts of kindness and defines the responsibilities and rights of various relationships. In a widening circle of relationships, then, our first obligation is to our immediate family—parents, husband or wife and children, then to other relatives, neighbors, friends and acquaintances, orphans and widows, the needy of the community, our fellow Muslims, all our fellow human beings, and animals.

1. *Parents:* Respect and care for parents is very much stressed in the Islamic teaching and is a very important part of a Muslim's expression of faith.

> Your Sustainer has decreed that you worship none but Him, and that you be kind to parents. Whether one or both of them attain old age in your lifetime, do not say to them a word of contempt nor repel them, but address them in terms of honor. And, out of kindness, lower to them the wing of humility and say: "My Sustainer!

Bestow on them Thy mercy, even as they cherished me in childhood." (17:23–24, also 31:14)

2. *Husband, wife and children:* God has made men responsible for their wives and children in the matters of providing them with necessities, creating and maintaining a religious atmosphere in the home, and for their education and welfare. Women are responsible for the domestic well-being of their husbands and children and for the training of children. Mutual love and trust, keeping private what is personal between them, forgiving one another's weaknesses, and affection, warmth and kindness to each other are enjoined on both husband and wife. Children are to be helpful, respectful and obedient to their parents.

Men shall take full care of women with the bounties which God has bestowed more abundantly on some of them than on others, and with what they may spend out of their possessions. And the righteous women are the devout ones, who guard the intimacy which God has (ordained to be) guarded. (4:34)

They [wives] are your garments and you are their garments. (2:187)

The Prophet (peace be on him) has said: Among the believers who show most perfect faith are those who have the best disposition and are kindest to their families.

3. *Other relatives:* These come next in the line of those for whom a Muslim has responsibility. God says concerning blood ties:

And render to the relatives their due rights, as (also) to those in want, and to the traveller; and do not squander your wealth in the manner of a spendthrift. (17:26)

They ask thee what they should spend (in charity). Say: Whatever of your wealth you spend shall be for the parents and for the near of kin and the orphans and the needy and the traveller; and whatever good you do, verily, God has full knowledge thereof. (2:215)

4. *Neighbors:* A person's character is seen in its true light by his neighbors. It is the duty of a Muslim to show particular kindness to his neighbors and to offer them as much help as he can.

The Prophet (peace be on him) has said: When your neighbors say you have done well, you have done well; and when you hear them say you have done ill, you have done ill.

The Prophet also said: He is not a believer who eats his fill when his neighbor beside him is hungry.

A Muslim family in New York City.

5. *Orphans and widows:* Orphans and widows, in every society, need special care and provision. Although a widow may be averse to remarriage with the thought of remaining faithful to her husband's memory, still it is recommended that she should marry again.

> The Prophet (peace be on him) has said: He who strives on behalf of a widow and a poor person is like one who strives in God's path.

Similarly, it is the responsibility of the nearest relatives to take care of orphans as they would care for their own children. If there are no relatives or if for any reason they do not assume responsibility for the bereaved child, it is the obligation of some other Muslim individual or organization to take care of the child as tenderly as possible.

> And they ask thee about orphans. Say: To improve their condition is best. And if you share their life, they are your brothers, for God distinguishes between him who spoils things and him who improves. (2:220, also 4:2, 6, 10, 127, and 17:34)

6. *Those in need: Zakat* (poor-due) is the Fourth Pillar of Islam, and it is obligatory upon every Muslim whose economic position qualifies him to pay it (see Reading 10). Apart from *Zakat,* charity is enjoined over and over again in Qur'an and *Hadith.* This means that to do what we can to help others who are in need is a very important and basic part of Islam. When Muslims of earlier times obeyed these injunctions faithfully, the general level of prosperity was at times so high that no one could be found who was in need of help from the *Zakat* funds.

Acts of charity, whether involving material help or any other sort of giving, should be done in a generous and kind spirit and not followed by words which humiliate or create a sense of obligation.

> Those who spend their wealth in the way of God and do not thereafter mar their gifts with reminders of their generosity and hurting [the feelings of the recipients] shall have their reward with their Sustainer, and no fear need they have, neither shall they grieve. Kind words and forgiveness are better than charity followed by injury; and God is Self-Sufficient, Forbearing. (2:262–263)

7. *Fellow Muslims:* Relationships among Muslims are of very great importance, for all Muslims throughout the world form one community of people submitting to God's laws and striving to

please Him, mutually helping one another toward the goals of Islam. All Muslims are brothers and sisters to one another, and their behavior to each other should be that of members of a family, full of kindness and consideration.

> Verily, the believers are one brotherhood. (49:10)

> And hold fast to God's bond, all together, and do not draw apart from one another. (3:103)

> The Prophet (peace be on him) has said: A Muslim is a Muslim's brother: he does not wrong him or abandon him. If anyone cares for his brother's need, God will care for his need; if anyone removes his brother's anxiety, God will remove from him one of the anxieties on the Day of Judgment; and if anyone conceals a Muslim's secrets, God will conceal his secrets on the Day of Judgment.

8. *Fellow men:* In God's sight a person is judged only by his intentions and his actions. Considerations of birth, national origin, racial background, material success, social status, and so on, all have no consequence in the sight of God. As Muslims, therefore, we should treat all persons with fairness and kindness without regard to any of these man-made distinctions and differences.

> O mankind! We have created you from a male and a female, and made you into races and tribes that you may know one another. Verily, the most honorable among you in the sight of God is the one who is most God-conscious. And God is All-Knowing, All-Aware. (49:13)

> The Prophet (peace be on him) has said: All creatures are God's creatures, and those dearest to God are the ones who treat His children kindly.

9. *Animals:* Kindness and good treatment should be extended to animals as well as to human beings. The Prophet (peace be on him) forbade Muslims to starve, torment or mutilate animals. This, however, is not a prohibition against killing animals for food, in as merciful a manner as possible, or against killing animals or insects which are harmful to man, such as snakes, scorpions, flies, mosquitoes, and so on.

> There is not an animal on the earth, nor a bird that flies on its wings, but are communities like you. (6:38)

ECONOMIC AFFAIRS

According to Islam, God is Owner of all things, including those which human beings use and enjoy: land, crops, forests, oceans, minerals, and all other natural resources of this earth. Man, as vice-gerent of God on earth, is only a trustee. Thus a Muslim looks upon his wealth and material possessions as gifts and bounties from God, to be spent in ways pleasing to Him—that is, for satisfying the needs of oneself and one's immediate family, one's parents and relatives, orphans, widows, the poor and needy of the community, and for striving in the path of God. The economic resources of a country are God's bounties to the people as a whole. These ought to be developed and utilized for the benefit of all the people and not merely for a few, and not to be diverted to uses which are harmful in any way. Sharing rather than exploiting, co-operation rather than competition, is the true spirit of Islam. That is why usury (interest on loans), gambling, hoarding, greed, covetousness, and using money in any way which is wasteful are among the things forbidden by God.

> And do not consume your wealth among yourselves wrongly, neither proffer it to the judges [as a bribe] so that you may sinfully consume a portion of (other) people's wealth, and that knowingly. (2:188)

> O you who believe! Do not devour usury, doubled and multiplied; but fear God, that you may prosper. (3:130)

> For God does not love those who are proud and boastful, those who are miserly or enjoin miserliness on others, or hide the bounties which God has bestowed on them . . . (4:36)

In business transactions, honesty, trustworthiness and fair dealing are duties to God. Cheating, concealing the defects of merchandise, or taking advantage of someone's ignorance are prohibited to Muslims.

Concerning honesty and fair dealings, God says:

> And if one of you deposits something on trust with another, let the trustee discharge his trust, and fear his Sustainer. (2:283)

> Give full measure when you measure, and weigh with a straight balance. That is the most fitting and most advantageous in the final determination. (17:35)

ADMINISTRATIVE AFFAIRS

Administrators and judges bear a great responsibility. Unless such persons have a consciousness of their obligations to God, it is possible that they may be swayed by pressure groups, self-interest or by their own prejudices and preferences to deviate from justice. God wishes to impress upon all human beings, whether they are responsible for a few persons or for a whole nation, that justice and fair dealing are duties to Him, and even national interest should not be allowed to interfere with this obligation.

> O you who believe! Be securers of justice, witnesses for God, and do not let the hatred of a people make you swerve to do wrong and depart from justice. Be just: that is nearer to God-consciousness; and fear God, for God is well-acquainted with all that you do. (5:9)

A mosque school in India.

While concern for the welfare of the people, justice and obedience to God's laws are the duty of a ruler or governing body, the ruled are in turn obliged to obey their ruler or government as long as it does not command them to do anything in disobedience to God's laws. The ruler or governing body is under obligation to consult with the people (or their representatives) in order to ascertain their views and needs.

And consult among yourselves to settle affairs. (42:38)

O you who believe! Obey God and the Messenger, and those who are charged with authority among you. (4:59)

The Prophet (peace be on him) has said: Hearing and obeying are the duty of a Muslim both regarding what he likes and what he dislikes, as long as he is not commanded to perform an act of disobedience to God, in which case he must neither hear nor obey.

JIHAD: STRIVING IN THE CAUSE OF GOD

Jihad is an abbreviated way of saying *jihad fi sabeel Allah,* which means "striving in God's cause." This includes such efforts as teaching, explaining and expounding the message of Islam to others, working against evil and corruption, and joining forces with individuals or groups in combating injustice, social inequity, illiteracy, poverty, disease and other human problems. God says:

Let there arise out of you a group of people inviting to all that is good, enjoining what is right, and forbidding what is wrong; they are the successful. (3:104)

Another aspect of striving in the path of God is emigration from a place where one is oppressed to such an extent that he cannot live and act as a Muslim to a place where this is possible.

To those who leave their homes in God's cause, after suffering oppression, We will assuredly give a goodly home in this world; but truly the reward of the Hereafter will be greater, if they only realized (this). (16:41)

There are occasions, however, when it becomes necessary to take up arms against oppressors or aggressors. While forbidding Muslims to commit aggression, God commands them to defend themselves against those who attack or oppress them.

And fight in God's cause against those who wage war upon you; but do not commit aggression; verily God does not love aggressors. (2:190)

CONCLUSION

The moral teachings of Islam may be viewed in terms of an individual's rights and obligations in relation to other individuals. Although, as a matter of style, we have emphasized obligations, it is clear that what is seen as one person's obligations to another can also be seen as the latter's right on the former.

It ought to be emphasized, however, that according to Islam the rights and obligations of an individual derive their authority from God and His prophet (peace be on him), and not from any man-made system of ethics. The conduct prescribed by the Islamic teachings has much in common with other systems of ethics, but the spirit is different. For example, it is not peculiar to Islam that it asks for fairness and honesty in business transactions. What is unique in Islam is that, by insisting that fairness and honesty are obligations to God, it transforms an economic principle into a moral one. A Muslim businessman, by being fair and honest, is not only benefitting from a sound business practice, but also deriving the spiritual benefit of following the commandment of God; while, if he cheats, he is not only violating his duty toward his fellow human beings but disobeying God as well.

In summary, then, the moral teachings of Islam define a person's obligations and rights in relation to others, emphasizing that every obligation to others is, at the same time, an obligation to God. These teachings outline basic principles of conduct, such as honesty, justice, kindness and charity, which are as applicable in twentieth-century North America as they were in seventh-century Arabia.

And thou shalt not find any change in the law of God. (35:43)

Wedding festivities in the town of Fez, Morocco.

READING 13
The Family Life*
HAMMUDAH ABDALATI

There have been many definitions and descriptions of the family. For our purpose, we shall adopt the following simplified definition. The family is a human social group whose members are bound together by the bond of blood ties and/or marital relationship.

The family bond entails mutual expectations of rights and obligations that are prescribed by religion, enforced by law, and observed by the group members. Accordingly, the family members share certain mutual commitments. These pertain to identity and provision, inheritance and counsel, affection for the young and security for the aged, and maximization of effort to ensure the family continuity in peace.

As can be clearly seen from this, the foundations of the family in Islam are blood ties and/or marital commitments. Adoption, mutual alliance, clientage, private consent to sexual intimacy, and "common law" or "trial" marriages do not institute a family in the Islamic sense. Islam builds the family on solid grounds that are capable of providing reasonable continuity, true security, and mature intimacy. . . .

Islam recognizes the religious virtue, the social necessity, and the moral advantages of marriage. The normal course of behavior for the Muslim individual is to be family oriented and to seek a

*From Hammudah Abdalati, *Islam in Focus* (Indianapolis, Ind.: American Trust Publications, 1975), pp. 113–19.

family of his own. Marriage and the family are central in the Islamic system. There are many passages in the Qur'an and statements by the Prophet which go as far as to say that when a Muslim marries, he has thereby perfected half his religion; so let him be God-minded and careful with the other half.

Muslim scholars have interpreted the Qur'an to mean that marriage is a religious duty, a moral safeguard, and a social commitment. As a religious duty, it must be fulfilled; but like all other duties in Islam, it is enjoined only upon those who are capable of meeting the responsibilities involved.

THE MEANING OF MARRIAGE

Whatever meanings people assign to marriage, Islam views it as a strong bond . . . a challenging commitment in the fullest sense of the word. It is a commitment to life itself, to society, and to the dignified, meaningful survival of the human race. It is a commitment that married partners make to one another as well as to God. . . . To paraphrase some Qur'anic verses, the call is addressed to mankind to be dutiful to God, Who created them from a single soul, and from it or of it created its mate, and from the two of them scattered abroad many men and women (4:1). It was God Who created mankind out of one living soul, and created of that soul a spouse so that he might find comfort and rest in her (7:107). And it is a sign of God that He has created for men, of themselves, mates to seek in their company peace and tranquillity, and has set between them mutual love and mercy. Surely, in that are signs for those who contemplate (30:21). Even at the most trying times of married life, and in the midst of legal disputes and litigation, the Qur'an reminds the parties of God's law; it commands them to be kind to one another, truly charitable toward one another, and above all dutiful to God.

It is noteworthy that the Islamic provisions of marriage apply to men and women equally. For example, if celibacy is not recommended for men, it is equally so for women. This is in recognition of the fact that women's needs are equally legitimate and are seriously taken into consideration. In fact, Islam regards marriage to be the normal, natural course for women just as it is for men. It may even be more so for women because it assures them, among other things, of relative economic security. This significant additional advantage for women does not, however, characterize marriage as a purely economic transaction. In fact, the least focal aspect of marriage in Islam is the economic factor, no matter how powerful this may be. The Prophet is reported to have said that a woman is ordinarily sought as wife for her wealth, for her beauty, for the nobility of her stock, or for her religious qualities; but blessed and fortunate is he who chooses his mate for piety in preference to everything else. The Qur'an commands marriage to the spouseless and the pious even though they may be poor and slaves (24:32). On the other hand, whatever dowry (marriage gifts) a man gives his prospective wife belongs to her; and whatever she may have acquired prior to or after marriage is hers alone. There is no *necessary* community of property of husbands and wives. Furthermore, it is the husband who is responsible for the maintenance and economic security of the family. . . .

THE PERMANENCE OF MARRIAGE

Because Islam considers marriage a very serious commitment, it has prescribed certain measures to make the marital bond as permanent as humanly possible. The parties must strive to meet the conditions of proper age, general compatibility, reasonable dowry, good will, free consent, unselfish guardianship, honorable intentions, and judicious discretion. When the parties enter into a marital contract, the intention must be clear to make the bond permanent, free from the casual and temporary designations. For this reason, trial marriages, term marriages, and all marriages that appear experimental, casual, or temporary are forbidden in Islam. In one of his most unequivocal statements, the Prophet declared that condemned are the men and women who relish the frequent change of marital partners, that is, the "tasters" who enjoy one partner for a while, then shift to another, then to a third, and so on.

However, to insist on the permanent character of marriage does not mean that the marital contract is absolutely indissoluble. Muslims are designated by the Qur'an as a Middle Nation and Islam is truly a religion of the "Golden Mean," the well-balanced and well-integrated system. This is particularly clear in the case of marriage which Islam regards as neither a sacrament nor a simple civil contract. Rather, marriage in Islam is something unique with very special features of both sacramental and contractural nature. It is equally true that the alternative to this casual or temporary extremity is not the other extreme of absolute indissolubility of the marital contract. The Islamic course is one of equitable and realistic moderation. The marriage contract should be taken as a serious, permanent bond. But if it does not work well for any valid reason, it may be terminated in kindness and honor, with equity and peace.

THE HUSBAND-WIFE RELATIONSHIP

With piety as the basis of mate selection, and with the earnest satisfaction of the conditions of marriage, the parties should be well on the way to a happy and fulfilling married life. However, Islam goes much further than this in setting the course of behavior for husbands and wives. Many are the statements of the Qur'an and the Sunnah that prescribe kindness and equity, compassion and love, sympathy and consideration, patience and good will. The Prophet goes as far as to declare that the best Muslim is the one who is best to his family, and the greatest, most blessed joy in life is a good, righteous wife.

The consummation of marriage creates new roles for the parties concerned. Each role is a set of equitable, proportionate rights and obligations. The role of the husband evolves around the moral principle that it is his solemn duty to God to treat his wife with kindness, honor, and patience; to keep her honorably or free her from the marital bond honorably; and to cause her no harm or grief (Qur'an, 2:229–232; 4:19). The role of the wife is summarized in the verse that women have rights even as they have duties, according to what is equitable. . . .

A. The Wife's Rights: The Husband's Obligations

Translated into rules of behavior, these ethical principles allocate to the wife certain rights and corresponding obligations. Because the Qur'an and the Sunnah of the Prophet have commanded kindness to women, it is the husband's duty to consort with his wife in an equitable and kind manner. One specific consequence of this Divine command is his responsibility for the full maintenance of the wife, a duty which he must discharge cheerfully, without reproach, injury, or condescendence.

A Moroccan husband and wife.

The wife's material rights are not her only assurances and securities. She has other rights of a moral nature; and they are equally binding and specific. A husband is commanded by the law of God to treat his wife with equity, to respect her feelings, and to show her kindness and consideration. She is not to be shown any aversion by the husband or subjected to suspense and uncertainty. A corollary of this rule is that no man is allowed to keep his wife with the intention of inflicting harm on her or hindering her freedom. If he has no love or sympathy for her, she has the right to demand freedom from the marital bond, and no one may stand in her way to a new life.

B. The Wife's Obligations: The Husband's Rights

The main obligation of the wife as a partner in a marital relationship is to contribute to the success and blissfulness of the marriage as much as possible. She must be attentive to the comfort and well-being of her mate. She may neither offend him nor hurt his feelings. Perhaps nothing can illustrate the point better than the Qur'anic statement which describes the righteous people as those who pray:

Our Lord! Grant unto us spouses and offspring who will be the joy and the comfort of our eyes, and guide us to be models of righteousness (Qur'an, 25:74).

This is the basis on which all the wife's obligations rest and from which they flow. To fulfill this basic obligation, the wife must be faithful, trustworthy, and honest. More specifically, she must not deceive her mate by deliberately avoiding conception lest it deprive him of legitimate progeny. Nor must she allow any other person to have access to that which is exclusively the husband's right, i.e., sexual intimacy. A corollary of this is that she must not receive or entertain strange males in her home without his knowledge and consent. Nor may she accept their gifts without his approval. . . .

. . . The wife is not expected to do anything that may render her companionship less desirable or less gratifying. If she does any such thing or neglects herself, the husband has the right to interfere with her freedom to rectify the situation. To insure maximum self-fulfillment for both partners, he is not permitted to do anything on his part that may impede her gratification.

READING 14
The Social System of Islam*
ZEBA SIDDIQUI

A sense of brotherliness pervades all the relationships of Muslims. Traditionally they address one another as "brother" and "sister," and try to behave accordingly. Responsibility may be said to be the keynote of Muslims' relationships with others. Their manners reflect an innate courtesy and consideration. They prefer their brothers or sisters in faith over themselves, and thanks or repayment are never expected in return for help or kindness. Generosity and hospitality are prized characteristics in Islam.

Muslims are expected to cooperate with each other rather than to compete. The Holy Qur'an says:

> Help one another in righteousness and piety, but do not help one another in sin and rancour. Fear God, for God is strict in punishment. (5:3)

Competition is stressed only when it is for excellence and good qualities and deeds.

> And vie with one another to attain your Sustainer's forgiveness and to a Paradise as vast as the heavens and the earth, which awaits the God-conscious, those who spend for charity in time of plenty and in time of hardship, and restrain their anger and pardon their fellow men, for God loves those who do good; who, when they have committed a shameful deed or have sinned against themselves, remember God and ask for forgiveness for their sins—for who but God could forgive sins?—and do not persist knowingly in doing

*From Zeba Siddiqui, "This Is Islam" (to be published by the Muslim Students' Association of the United States and Canada).

whatever (wrong) they did. These it is who shall have as their reward forgiveness from their Sustainer and Gardens through which running waters flow, therein to abide. How excellent a reward for those who labor. (3:133–136)

Islam enjoins mutual helpfulness and consideration. If people are in need or difficulty, Muslims are expected to help them materially or with moral support. Pride and a sense of being superior to others are among the most condemnable sins, and Muslims are supposed to be genuinely humble and modest no matter what their attainments may be. In a well-known *Hadith,* the Prophet referred to Muslims as the "mirror" of one another. Thus another form of helping one's fellow Muslims is to restrain them from wrong acts, and "enjoining what is right and forbidding what is evil" (3:104, 110) is a fundamental duty.

Islam permits and encourages free enterprise and trade, and all members of the society are allowed to earn in accordance with their skills. Muslims' charitableness helps equalize the wealth in the society and produces a sense of brotherhood and mutual love among the well-to-do and the less fortunate. All Muslims are expected to feel and to accept responsibility for those they are close to or associated with. For example, orphans are cared for by relatives if they have any, not put into institutions. A similar responsibility is assumed for widows, divorced women, the handicapped, and the aged by their relatives. Muslims have various responsibilities to the individuals who make up the society, as well as to God, to themselves, and to their families. In other words, Islamic virtues such as charitableness and kindness are personalized rather than institutionalized and are the responsibility of every member of the society.

In any group of three or more Muslims, one is selected as the leader. This applies not only to a group which has gathered for *Salat* but to any group, including a Muslim country or a Muslim family (in which the husband is the leader). The other members are supposed to obey their leader, even if they disagree with him, unless he asks them to do something which involves disobedience to God. In this case they are entitled to reason with the leader and try to convince him that another course is better than the one he has chosen. But whether they agree with him or not, they must obey him since he is the one to whom they have delegated leadership and authority. However, if he fails in his responsibilities or asks them to do something that is against Islam, he should be replaced. The leader, for his part, must consult with the people and consider their needs and wishes as far as possible.

Islam is not a religion for the individual alone but for the society as well. For Islam intends that societies, as well as individuals, be based on righteousness and the fear of God. An ideal Islamic society, in which all legislation is based on the Qur'an, the Prophet's practice, and certain other accepted Islamic legal principles, would have the following characteristics:

It should provide the proper religious and social climate for its people. It would provide and maintain mosques and schools, and

Muslims in typical Moroccan dress greet each other on a street in Tetouan.

pay the salaries of teachers and religious functionaries. The Islamic society should make it easy for Muslims to practice Islam and also difficult for them to deviate from it. In an Islamic state or society, gambling, drinking, and drug use would be illegal and punishable, as would prostitution, sexual relations outside marriage, and homosexuality. Night clubs, dance halls, bars, and mixed swimming facilities would not be allowed. Pornographic literature and degrading television programs and movies would not be permitted.

However, Islam is much more than merely a series of prohibitions. More importantly, it is a positive program of life for the well-being of individuals and their society. In an Islamic society, religious education in a broad sense would be available and compulsory. Such education would present Islam as a dynamic system for the total life of individuals and the society, and a sense of pride in one's Islamic identity and heritage would be reinforced by all possible means. Facilities for adult education should be provided as well, and parents should be given every support and encouragement in the proper rearing of their children. The dignity and honor of women, including separation of the sexes wherever necessary (public transportation, secondary schools, medical and sports facilities, etc.), should be protected, and a proper and dignified Islamic dress should be encouraged. Young people should be helped to marry early so that their sex drives may be met without resorting to illicit behavior. Family stability and well-being should be fostered by every possible means. Suitable sports, recreations, and entertainments consistent with Islamic standards should also be encouraged.

Social justice for all inhabitants of an Islamic society is required by Islam, whether they are Muslims or non-Muslims. Islam guarantees freedom of religion and conscience to non-Muslims living in such a society. The Qur'an explicitly orders, "Let there be no compulsion in religion" (2:256), since one's religion is obviously a matter of inner conviction. However, non-Muslims living in an Islamic state would be required to conform to some extent and would not be permitted to engage in activities prohibited by Islam. No open or implied discrimination on the basis of race, color, or nationality would be tolerated.

This, then, is the ideal of an Islamic society—a society in which, Muslims believe, human dignity is raised to the highest level. For

Islam calls for a society in which individuals attain their maximum capacity as *human* beings having material, moral, and spiritual needs and characteristics. Islam integrates these, both in the individual and in the society, since there is no division caused by applying different values and criteria to different aspects of life. Although such an ideal Islamic society, as Muslims themselves admit only too readily, does not exist anywhere in the world at the present time, it did exist, as a matter of historical record, in the early times of Islam when Islam was applied as a total and complete system of life.

One must therefore always bear in mind that it is the Islamic ideal and standard, rather than the behavior of individuals or societies, which is the criterion. That standard will always remain the same, regardless of whether it is followed or disregarded, for it comes from Almighty God. Thus it is eternal and without change for all time to come, and is entirely independent of the actions of human beings. Muslims believe this standard is as relevant and applicable today, and at any time past or present, as it was when the Prophet brought it fourteen hundred years ago. Whether they come close to it or fall short of it, it is this standard and ideal that Muslims refer to in all their actions. And it is toward this ideal that Islamic leaders throughout the world today are directing their efforts in trying to bring about a revival of Islam.

Today a sizable number of Muslims live in various countries of the West. It is estimated that there are roughly three million Muslims in the United States and Canada and eighteen million in various countries of Europe. Of these, a large number are students from all parts of the Muslim world; another large group is formed by emigrants; and the third group consists of native Muslim converts.

In the major cities of almost every country of the Western world today there are Islamic centers or mosques which serve the needs of the Muslim communities. Many of these have permanent salaried directors, or *imams.* Many provide classes in Islam for children, and attend to community functions such as marriages, funerals, Friday prayers and in some cases the five daily prayers, and celebration of Islamic holidays and occasions. In addition, the centers are a focus for the Muslim community, helping its members to keep their Islamic identity and traditions and to propagate Islam among Muslims and non-Muslims alike.

Working in an oil refinery in the Persian Gulf State of Bahrain.

READING 15
Other Aspects of Daily Life*
ZEBA SIDDIQUI

WORK

In Islam the broad meaning of worship is not confined to so-called religious observances such as praying and fasting, for Islam does not acknowledge any distinction between the sacred and worldly aspects of existence. Thus everything which is done in a lawful manner to satisfy one's legitimate needs and those of one's family with the intention of pleasing God is considered as worship. This is why Islam is always referred to as a *deen*—that is, a way of life—rather than a religion in the usual sense. Work, too, is a part of the Muslim's worship in this broad sense.

Islam is not a lazy person's religion. Obviously a strong sense of discipline and considerable effort are required to observe prayers at their proper times and to fast throughout a whole month. The need to work hard in one's area of responsibility is also strongly stressed.

In Islam all legitimate work is considered respectable, from manual labor to the highest intellectual and scientific achievement. Although Islam has established *Zakat* to help people who cannot meet their own needs, it nevertheless strongly discourages begging or living off the contributions of others. In fact, *Zakat* is to be given to those who do *not* ask for it. A *Hadith* of the

*From Zeba Siddiqui, "This Is Islam" (to be published by the Muslim Students' Association of the United States and Canada).

Prophet emphasizes the respectability of work in the following words: "It is better for one of you to take his rope, bring a load of firewood on his back and sell it, God thereby preserving his self-respect, than that he should beg from people, whether they give him anything or refuse him." The Prophet set the example by doing various kinds of manual labor and household work himself.

Thus every member of the Muslim community must contribute his or her efforts and skills for the good of the society, whether within the home or in the outside world. "That man shall have nothing but what he strives for" (53:39) summarizes Islam's attitude toward work and worldly striving.

MONEY AND POSSESSIONS

While Islam permits and even encourages ownership of property and wealth, it stresses that wealth is merely a convenience—a tool for living in this world. Thus, while wealth can be earned and enjoyed, it is not to become the focus of one's life or an end in itself. Rather, wealth is a means to the end of fulfilling one's Islamic obligations and living a life which is pleasing to God. Muslims, therefore, regard money and everything they have—time, talents, health, and possessions—as gifts and trusts from God. They are not theirs by right or simply due to their own efforts, but a mercy and a bounty from Almighty God. As such, devout Muslims appreciate the wealth God has given them, whether it is much or little, and try to find the best uses for it. In addition to being used for themselves and their families, their wealth is to be spent for others and for Islam.

Giving and taking interest is not permitted by Islam, and Muslims are expected to find workable alternatives to this practice. Money is to be kept in circulation by expenditure or investment rather than simply saved, as its purpose is to be used for the benefit of the society rather than sitting idle. On a personal level, Islam stresses generosity and open-handedness. At the same time, it discourages extravagant spending, hoarding, wasting, spending to impress others, and miserliness. Muslims are supposed to be moderate and reasonable in their demands and flexible in their living habits, so that whether they are rich or poor they will be content and thankful for whatever God has given them.

FOOD AND DRINK

Certain foods are forbidden to Muslims. The rule is that whatever is not specifically or by analogy prohibited is permissible. The foods and drinks which Islam prohibits are (1) intoxicants and drugs, in any quantity, (2) pork and its by-products, (3) the flesh of animals which have died without being slaughtered, (4) animals killed by a blow, by falling, or being gored with horns, (5) birds of prey, rodents, reptiles, and animals with claws, (6) blood, and (7) anything dedicated to, or killed in the name of, a deity other than God.

Muslims slaughter an animal by slitting its throat, saying *Bismillah* ("In the name of God"). This acknowledges that the life of this creature of God is taken only by His permission to meet the lawful need for food. All the blood is then drained. While some Muslims eat the meat which is slaughtered commercially in non-Muslim countries, others do not eat meat which is not slaughtered by Muslims or in the Kosher manner. Many Muslim communities in the West today make such meat available.

Islam's attitude toward food embodies its attitude toward all the good things of this life. Food is not something to be taken for granted, but to be accepted thankfully as the bounty of God. It is to be enjoyed and used wisely and for maximum benefit, not for self-indulgence. Wasting food is considered a sin, as it is to be treated as a precious gift from God.

A *Hadith* of the Prophet says that one-third of the stomach is for food, one-third for drink, and one-third for air. Again, the Prophet said that Muslims are those who do not eat unless they are hungry, and when they eat, they do not fill themselves. This points to moderation in food habits and to the desirability of eating to maintain physical well-being, rather than simply to satisfy one's appetite. Food is to be shared, and Muslims consider it a blessing to have guests to join the meal. Good manners, consideration of others, and appropriate conversation should accompany it. Meals begin with the words *Bismillah ar-Rahman ar-Raheem* ("In the name of God, the Beneficent, the Merciful") and end with brief words of thanksgiving.

DRESS

The dress of Muslim women is not an isolated aspect of life but fits into and reinforces the social system of Islam. It is closely connected with the Islamic view of womanhood and Islam's strong emphasis on purity and chastity. The dress which Islam prescribes for Muslim women neutralizes their sexual attributes and keeps them from being a source of temptation to men.

Islam requires men to cover at least the area between the navel and the knee. Women must cover the entire body except the hands and face. (In many parts of the Muslim world women cover their faces as well, for even greater modesty.) No specific dress is prescribed, but women's clothing should not merely cover. It should also be loose enough to conceal the shape, should be nontransparent, and should not attract attention by its beauty. The Qur'an asks women not to display their "ornaments," both natural and artificial, in front of men. Thus makeup, jewelry, and beautiful clothing are permitted only in the presence of one's husband, immediate family, or other women. The Muslim woman makes herself beautiful for her husband rather than for outsiders. She wears what she likes in the privacy of her home and observes strict modesty outside. Ideally, the dress of Muslim women should not imitate the dress of non-Muslims, nor does it need to imitate the dress of past times or of other countries. Rather, Muslims are expected to retain their own identity and to keep, or originate, their own forms of dress.

LEISURE-TIME ACTIVITIES

Because Islam is a system governing the totality of human life, not merely some particular aspects of it, it obviously has something to say about how Muslims spend their free time. For Islam teaches that a person's life, with all its resources of time, energy, skills, health, and possessions, is given to him or her for the purpose of serving and pleasing God, and that God has defined the proper uses of all these gifts. Thus Muslims are expected to consider whether their activities make suitable use of God's gifts. This of course does not mean that Muslims are never supposed to enjoy themselves or have any entertainments, recreations, sports, or interests. It merely means that whatever these activities and interests are, they should help Muslims achieve their primary goal of living God-conscious lives in obedience to the teachings of Islam.

This approach eliminates many activities because of their unsuitable content. Others are not permissible because of their

A Muslim woman in the Yemen Arab Republic is modestly clothed in veils.

form—for example, mixed swimming and mixed dancing of any type. There are a few additional restrictions for women, such as singing in public or taking part in dramas or other public entertainments which focus male attention on their persons. However, such activities are permissible in an all-female group.

For many other activities, there is no clear-cut rule. The Muslim is expected to determine whether an activity fits in with the Islamic frame of reference and values, and whether it will contribute in any way to living an Islamic life or to the benefit of one's family. Apart from purely recreational uses of leisure, the Muslim may wish to spend his or her free time working for good causes of various types and spreading the message of Islam, which is an obligation on all who profess Islam.

PART IV
Summary of Islam

As the readings in this book have confirmed, Islam is not a mere belief system. Nor is it a religion in the usual sense of the word. Rather, it is a way of life—a total system which governs all aspects of a Muslim's life. To summarize the Islamic tradition, Part IV presents two readings, one on the concept of faith in Islam and the other on the meaning of Islam.

A Muslim reads inside the Mosque of the Olive Tree in Tunisia.

READING 16
The Concept of Faith (Iman)*
HAMMUDAH ABDALATI

Some people may think that man becomes a Muslim when he confesses belief in the Oneness of the True God and in Muhammad as His Last Messenger. But this is far from the full meaning of Faith. The full meaning of Faith in Islam is not, by any means, something nominal or mere formality. Faith in Islam is a state of happiness acquired by virtue of positive action and constructive conceptions as well as dynamic and effective measures.

The Holy Qur'an and the Traditions of Muhammad define these required measures and establish the standards which build up a meaningful Faith. Thus, the true believers are:

1. Those who believe in God, His angels, His Books as completed by the Qur'an, His messengers with Muhammad being the Last of them all, the Day of Final Judgment, the absolute knowledge and wisdom of God.

2. Those who trust God always and enjoy unshakable confidence in Him.

3. Those who spend in the way of God of what He has given them in the form of wealth, life, health, knowledge, experience, and so on.

4. Those who observe their daily prayers regularly as well as the weekly and annual congregations.

5. Those who pay their religious taxes (alms or Zakah) to the rightful beneficiaries (individuals or institutions), the *minimum* of

*From Hammudah Abdalati, *Islam in Focus* (Indianapolis, Ind.: American Trust Publications, 1975), pp. 23–25.

which is two and a half percent of the annual "net" income, or of the total value of stocks [inventory] if in business—after discounting all expenses and credits.

6. Those who enjoin the right and good, and combat the wrong and evil by all lawful means at their disposal.

7. Those who obey God and His Messenger Muhammad; and feel increasing strength of faith when the Qur'an is recited, and humility of heart when God's name is mentioned.

8. Those who love God and His Messenger most, and love their fellow men sincerely for the sake of God alone.

9. Those who love their near and distant neighbors and show genuine kindness to their guests, especially the strangers.

10. Those who say the truth and engage in good talk, or else abstain.

It is clear that the very meaning of Faith makes Islam penetrate deeply and constructively into every aspect of life. According to Islam, true Faith has a decisive effect on the spiritual and material lot of man, and also on his personal and social behaviour as well as his political conduct and financial life. To show how the Qur'an describes the true believers, here are some examples. The Qur'an contains numerous references like these:

They only are the true believers whose hearts feel submissive (and humble) when God is mentioned; and when the revelations of God are recited unto them, they (the revelations) increase and strengthen their Faith; and who trust in their Lord, establish the prayer (as enjoined on them) and spend of what We have bestowed on them (in the cause of God). Those are they who are in truth believers. For them are (high) grades (of honor) with their Lord, and a bountiful provision (Qur'an, 8:2–4).

And the believers, men and women, are protecting (and allied) friends of one another; they enjoin the right and forbid the wrong, and they establish worship and they pay the poor-due, and they obey God and His Messenger. As for these, God will have mercy on them; verily God is Mighty, and Wise. God promises the believers, men and women, Gardens under which rivers flow, to dwell therein, and beautiful mansions in Gardens of everlasting bliss. But the greatest bliss is the Good Pleasure of God. That is the supreme felicity (Qur'an, 9:71–72).

The true believers are those only who believe in God and His Messenger (Muhammad) and afterward doubt not, but strive with their wealth and their lives for the cause of God. Such are the sincere (Qur'an, 49:15).

Besides these Qur'anic references, there are many relevant Traditions of Muhammad. For example, he says:

None of you can be a true believer unless he loves for his fellow believer what he loves for himself.

Three qualities are the sign of sound faith, and he who acquires them can really feel the sweet taste of Faith. They are (1) to love God and His Messenger most of all, (2) to love his fellow man for the sake of God alone, and (3) to resent and resist returning to disbelief as much as he does being cast into fire.

He who believes in God and the Last Day of Judgment is forbidden to cause any harm to his neighbor, is to be kind to his guests—especially the strangers, and is to say the truth or else abstain.

Muslims pray in the Blue Mosque in Istanbul, Turkey.

READING 17

The Meaning of Islam*

HAMMUDAH ABDALATI

The word Islam is derived from the Arabic root "SLM" which means, among other things, peace, purity, submission and obedience. In the religious sense the word Islam means submission to the Will of God and obedience to His Law. The connection between the original and the religious meanings of the word is strong and obvious. Only through submission to the Will of God and by obedience to His Law can one achieve true peace and enjoy lasting purity.

Some outsiders call our religion "Mohammedanism" and address the believers in Islam as "Mohammedans". The Muslims both reject and protest the use of these words. If our faith is classified as Mohammedanism and if we are called Mohammedans, there will be seriously wrong implications. This misnomer implies that the religion takes its name after a mortal being, namely, Muhammad and that Islam is no more than another "ism" just like Judaism, Hinduism, Marxism, etc. Another wrong implication of this misnomer is that outsiders might think of the Muslims, whom they call Mohammedans, as worshippers of Muhammad or as believers in him in the same way as Christians, for example, believe in Jesus. A further wrong implication is that the word Mohammedanism may mislead the outsider and make him think that the religion was founded by Muhammad and therefore takes its name after the founder. All these implications

*From Hammudah Abdalati, *Islam in Focus,* pp. 7–9.

are seriously wrong or at best misleading. Islam is not just another "ism". Nor do Muslims worship Muhammad or look upon him the same way as Christians, Jews, Hindus, Marxists, etc., look upon their respective leaders. The Muslims worship God alone. Muhammad was only a mortal being commissioned by God to teach the word of God and lead an exemplary life. He stands in history as the best model for man in piety and perfection. He is a living proof of what man can be and of what he can accomplish in the realm of excellence and virtue. Moreover, the Muslims do not believe that Islam was founded by Muhammad, although it was restored by him in the last stage of religious evolution. The original founder of Islam is no other than God Himself, and the date of the founding of Islam goes back to the age of Adam. Islam has existed in one form or another all along from the beginning and will continue to exist till the end of time.

The true name of the religion, then, is Islam and those who follow it are Muslims. Contrary to popular misconceptions, Islam or submission to the Will of God, together with obedience to His Law, does not mean in any way loss of individual freedom or surrender to fatalism. Anyone who thinks or believes so has certainly failed to understand the true meaning of Islam and the concept of God in Islam. The concept of God in Islam describes Him as the Most Merciful and Gracious, and the Most Loving and most concerned with the well-being of man, and as Full of Wisdom and care for His Creatures. His Will, accordingly, is a Will of Benevolence and Goodness, and whatever Law He prescribes must be in the best interest of mankind.

When the civilized people abide by the laws of their countries, they are considered sound citizens and honest members of their respective societies. No responsible person would say that such people lose their freedom by their obedience to the Law. No rational being would think or believe for a moment that such law-abiding people are fatalists and helpless. Similarly, the person who submits to the Will of God, which is a good Will, and obeys the Law of God, which is the best Law, is a sound and honest person. He is gaining protection of his own rights, showing genuine respect for the rights of others, and enjoying a high degree of responsible, creative freedom. Submission to the good Will of God, therefore, does not take away or curtail individual freedom. On the contrary, it gives freedom of a high degree in abundant measures. It frees the mind from superstitions and fills it with truth. It frees the soul from sin and wrong and quickens it with goodness and purity. It frees the self from vanity and greed, from envy and tension, from fear and insecurity. It frees man from subjugation to false deities and low desires, and unfolds before him the beautiful horizons of goodness and excellence.

Submission to the good Will of God, together with obedience to His beneficial Law, is the best safeguard of peace and harmony. It enables man to make peace between himself and his fellow men on the one hand, and between the human community and God on the other. It creates harmony among the elements of Nature. According to Islam, everything in the world, or every phenomenon other than man is administered by God-made Laws. This makes the entire physical world necessarily obedient to God and submissive to His Laws, which, in turn, means that it is in a state of Islam, or it is Muslim. The physical world has no choice of its own. It has no voluntary course to follow on its own initiative but obeys the Law of the Creator, the Law of Islam or submission. Man alone is singled out as being endowed with intelligence and the power of making choices. And because man possesses the qualities of intelligence and choice he is invited to submit to the good Will of God and obey His Law. When he does choose the course of submission to the Law of God, he will be making harmony between himself and all the other elements of Nature, which are by necessity obedient to God. He will be consistent with the truth and in harmony with all the other elements of the universe. But if he chooses disobedience he will deviate from the Right Path and will be inconsistent. Besides, he will incur the displeasure and punishment of the Law-Giver.

Because Islam means submission to the Good Will of God and obedience to His Beneficial Law, and because this is the essence of the message of all God-chosen messengers, a Muslim accepts all the prophets previous to Muhammad without discrimination. He believes that all those prophets of God and their faithful followers were Muslims, and that their religion was Islam, the only true universal religion of God (Qur'an, 2:128–140; 3:78–85; 17:42–44; 31:22; 42:13).

Artistically written in the center of the ceiling of the Omayyad Mosque in Damascus are the words: "Everyone acts according to his own disposition. . . ." (Qur'an 17:84)

Glossary

Definitions are limited to those that apply to usage of words and phrases within this book. Italic words in the definitions are defined elsewhere in the Glossary.

Abdullah. *Muhammad*'s father, who died shortly before Muhammad was born.

Abdul Muttalib. *Muhammad*'s grandfather, who looked after Muhammad for a time after his father died and who rediscovered the Well of *Zamzam.*

Abraham. Father of *Ishmael* and Isaac and one of the patriarchs of the Old Testament. In Arabic, "Ibrahim."

Abu Bakr. A close companion of *Muhammad* who became one of his disciples and eventually accompanied him from *Mecca* to *Medina.* In 632 he succeeded Muhammad as the leader of the Muslim community and became the first Muslim *caliph.* He was known as "al-Siddiq," that is, "truthful."

Abu Bakr Siddiq. See *Abu Bakr.*

Abu Sufyan. A Meccan leader who suffered defeat at the hands of the *Prophet*'s army in the Battle of *Badr* in 624.

Abu Talib. *Muhammad*'s paternal uncle and guardian after the age of nine or ten, who eventually took Muhammad to *Palestine* and Syria.

Abyssinia. Former name of the country of Ethiopia.

Adam. The first man created by God; the first of all *prophets,* the last of whom is *Muhammad* according to *Islam.*

Adhan. The first call to prayers *(salat)* given when *Muslims* meet as a congregation.

'Aisha. Daughter of *Abu Bakr* and one of *Muhammad*'s wives. After Muhammad's death, she became recognized as an authority on his life and teachings.

Al-Amin. A title given to *Muhammad* meaning "the faithful one."

Al-Ghazzali. A Muslim theologian and philosopher of the eleventh and twelfth centuries.

Ali. *Muhammad*'s cousin and son-in-law (son of *Abu Talib*), who embraced *Islam* in early youth.

Allah. The Arabic name for "the one God."

Al-Marwa. One of two small hills in *Mecca* where *Hagar* and *Ishmael* found water when they were perishing. See *As-Safa.*

Amanah. Honesty—one of the four virtues ascribed to the *prophets* of *Islam.*

Amina bint Wahb. *Muhammad*'s mother, wife of *Abdullah,* who died when her son was about six years of age.

Angel Gabriel. See *Gabriel, Angel.*

Ansars. A name given to the Medinites who gave refuge to the *Prophet* and his disciples and became known as their "helpers."

Arabs. Semitic peoples originally inhabiting the Arabian Peninsula.

Arafat, Mount. A hill near *Mecca* where pilgrims go during *hajj* to worship, repent for their sins, and reaffirm their brotherhood.

Articles of Faith. The various beliefs which a *Muslim* must subscribe to. These include beliefs in the oneness of God, the revealed books, the *prophets,* the angels, the hereafter, and *Qadar.*

'Asr. The late afternoon prayer, consisting of four *rakat* said silently.

As-Safa. One of the two small hills in *Mecca* where *Hagar* and *Ishmael* found water when they were perishing. See *Al-Marwa.*

Attributes (of God). According to the *Qur'an* the attributes, or characteristics, of God are: Almighty, Omnipresent, Eternal, Transcendent, and Immanent.

Badr, Battle of. The first of *Muhammad*'s battles, fought in 624, in which the *Muslims* routed the Meccans under *Abu Sufyan* and interrupted their trade with Syria and other parts of the Near East. Badr was located near the Red Sea, southwest of *Medina.*

Bait-al-Mal. Exchequer, or state treasury.

Bedouin. Members of one of the nomadic, desert-dwelling tribes of the Arabian Peninsula and North Africa.

Book, The. To *Muslims,* the Holy *Qur'an.*

Caliph. The head of a Muslim community, recognized as both a temporal and spiritual leader of *Islam.*

Christianity. The religion that teaches that God is the creator and sustainer of the universe and *Jesus* Christ is its lord and savior.

Commandments, Ten. The injunctions given to *Moses* by God outlining ethical behavior toward God and one's neighbors.

Creed. A statement of religious belief.

David. An Old Testament king who was responsible for unifying the ancient Hebrews and building an Israelite kingdom. He was also the author of the biblical songs known as the *Psalms* ("Zabur").

Day of Judgment. The end of the world, when all will be raised up in physical form and be rewarded or punished by God according to their intentions and actions in this life.

Deen. A way of life; for *Muslims,* all life lived in accordance with Islamic teaching.

Dhimmis. Non-*Muslims* living in Islamic states.

Dhul-Hijja. The twelfth month of the Islamic calendar, during which the *hajj* takes place.

Dhul-Qu'da. The eleventh month of the Islamic calendar.

Ditch, Battle of. An unsuccessful attack by the Meccans and their Jewish allies on the *Muslims* at *Medina* in 627, so called because the *Prophet* directed a ditch be built to protect the city.

Du'a. Nonprescribed, private prayers to God whenever one wishes.

Dualism. The belief that the universe is under the influence of both a good principle and an evil principle.

Eid. A day of thanksgiving and rejoicing after fulfilling the obligation of fasting.

Eid-ul-Adha. The Festival of Sacrifice observed during *hajj* and elsewhere in the Muslim world during which the faithful sacrifice a sheep, a goat, or a camel in honor of God's having released *Abraham* from the sacrifice of his son *Ishmael.*

Eid-ul-Fitr. The Festival of Fast Breaking, occurring on the first day of *Shawwal,* right after *Ramadan.*

Fajr. The dawn prayer, consisting of two *rakat* said aloud.

Fard. Prescribed and obligatory prayers in Muslim ritual; any strict obligation which should not be omitted.

Farthest Mosque. The Muslim place of worship built on the site of *Solomon's Temple* in Jerusalem, often visited by pilgrims during *hajj.*

Fatanah. Intelligence—one of the four virtues ascribed to the *prophets* of Islam.

Five Pillars of Islam. See *Pillars of Islam, Five.*

Gabriel, Angel. God's messenger who revealed the Holy *Qur'an* to *Muhammad.* In Arabic, "Jibril."

Ghassanids. Inhabitants of an ancient Arabian kingdom in present-day Syria which was conquered by the *Muslims* around 632.

Habash. An ancient country in what is now Ethiopia (formerly *Abyssinia*).

Hadith. A saying of the *Prophet;* teachings conveyed by the Prophet to his followers in his own words.

Hagar. *Abraham*'s wife, mother of *Ishmael.*

Hajj. An annual pilgrimage to *Mecca* at a specified time which every practicing *Muslim* must make at least once in his or her lifetime if at all possible.

Hajju at-tamattu'. The "interrupted pilgrimage," which permits a *Muslim* to arrive early in *Mecca*, perform a minor pilgrimage, then wait to perform the major pilgrimage at the later specified time.

Halima Saadiya. *Muhammad's Bedouin* foster-mother.

Hanif. Pure faith—the natural tendency of humans to believe in one God and perform good deeds.

Hijrah. The migration of *Muhammad* and his followers from *Mecca* to *Medina* in 622.

Hijrat. See *Hijrah.*

Hilm. An important virtue in Muslim interpersonal relationships meaning forbearance, kindness, and forgiveness.

Hinduism. The principle religion of India consisting of numerous cults and mystical practices and emphasizing the role of dharma (duty) in human life.

Hira. A cave near *Mecca* where *Muhammad* often used to go to think and pray.

Hudaibiya, Pact of. An agreement drawn up in 628 between the Meccans and *Muhammad* which allowed the *Prophet* to preach and make conversions as well as to permit *Muslims* to observe the *hajj* ceremonies in *Mecca.*

Ibrahim. See *Abraham.*

Iftar. The breaking of the *Ramadan* fast at sunset.

Ihram. The "pilgrim's dress" worn by men during pilgrimage to *Mecca*, consisting of two simple pieces of white cloth covering the upper and lower parts of the body.

Imam. A leader of a Muslim community who often directs the congregation in *salat.*

Iman. The *creed;* what a *Muslim* is supposed to believe in; points of creed.

Injil. Revelation given to *Jesus;* the New Testament.

Iqamah. The second call to prayer *(salat)* given when *Muslims* meet as a congregation.

'Isa. See *Jesus.*

'Isha. The night prayer, consisting of four *rakat,* two to be said aloud and two silently.

Ishmael. *Abraham*'s son by *Hagar* and, according to Muslim tradition, the father of the north Arabian tribes. In Arabic, "Isma'il."

Islam. The religion of the *Muslims,* meaning "peace" or "submission" to the will of God and obedience to His law.

Isma'il. See *Ishmael.*

Jahannum. "Hell" in Arabic.

Jannat. "Heaven" in Arabic.

Jesus. According to *Islam,* one of the *prophets,* or messengers, of God; according to some Christians, the Son of God and savior of the world. In Arabic, " 'Isa."

Jews. Those who follow the religion of *Judaism;* descendents of the Hebrews who lived in the ancient land of *Palestine* during the last few centuries before Christ; members of the tribe of Judah; Israelites.

Jibril. See *Gabriel, Angel.*

Jihad. The Muslim obligation to teach, explain, and spread the message of *Islam* and to combat evil and corruption even to the extent of defensive armed combat; a "striving in God's cause."

Judaism. The religion of the *Jews,* characterized by a belief in one God and adherence to the Scriptures and rabbinical tradition.

Julus. A ritual prayer position of sitting with legs folded under the body.

Jum'a. Friday, when congregational prayer is obligatory for *Muslims.*

Ka'aba (also spelled "Ka'bah"). The first house of worship of one God in *Mecca,* built by *Abraham* and *Ishmael* and restored to its purity by

Muhammad; the small shrine located in the center of *Mecca's* Great Mosque which is a place of pilgrimage for *Muslims.*

Ka'bah. See *Ka'aba.*

Khadijah. Muhammad's first wife and first convert to Islam.

Khalil-ul-Allah. A title given to *Abraham,* meaning "the friend of God."

Khaybar, Battle of. *Muhammad's* last battle against the *Jews* in which he captured their important oasis settlement in southwestern Saudi Arabia in 628.

Khutba. The sermon, or homily, addressed to the congregation by an *imam* on Friday or on *Eid-ul-Fitr* and *Eid-ul-Adha.*

Koran. See *Qur'an.*

Kosher. A ritually approved manner of slaughtering animals or birds.

Kufr. Nonbelief; denial of God.

Lailat-ul-Qadr. See *Night of Power, The.*

Maghrib. The evening or sunset prayer, consisting of three *rakat,* two said aloud and one said silently.

Manasik. Rituals.

Mecca. The holy city of *Islam* in west-central Saudi Arabia where *Muhammad* was born and to which the faithful make pilgrimage to visit the *Ka'aba.*

Medina. A city located almost due north of *Mecca* where the *Prophet* and his followers migrated in 622. Pilgrims today visit *Muhammad's* tomb and *mosque* in the city.

Messengers. See *Prophets.*

Mina. A village between *Mecca* and Mount *Arafat* where *Ishmael* resisted Satan's temptation to rebel against his father. Pilgrims on *hajj* visit the village and throw stones at pillars representing Satan to show their rejection of evil.

Mohammed. See *Muhammad.*

Moses. The great *prophet* of the Old Testament to whom God revealed the *Ten Commandments;* one of the *messengers* of God according to *Islam.* In Arabic, "Musa."

Mosque. A Muslim place of public worship.

Muezzin. One who calls a Muslim congregation to prayers *(salat).*

Muhammad. Founder of the religion of *Islam* and the *Prophet,* or *messenger* of God; born in *Mecca* in 570 and died in *Medina* in 632.

Muharram. First month of the Islamic calendar.

Mur'uwah. Nobility of character.

Musa. See *Moses.*

Muslims. Followers of the religion of *Islam.*

Muzdalifa. A town near Mount *Arafat* where pilgrims adjourn to recite certain prayers and spend the night during *hajj.*

Nabi. "Prophet," one of the names given to each of the twenty-five *messengers* mentioned in the Qur'an.

Night of Power, The. The night during *Ramadan* on which *Muhammad* first received the Divine message from the Angel *Gabriel.*

Niyat. Intention rather than actual performance in observance of a ritual.

Noah. A patriarch of the Old Testament who, in accordance with God's commands, perpetuated the human race and animal species by harboring them in the ark during the Deluge. In Arabic, "Nuh."

Nuh. See **Noah.**

Omar ibn al Khattab. A Meccan who was converted to *Islam* in 615 and later became the second Muslim *caliph,* following *Abu Bakr.*

Paganism. The worship of many gods; heathenism; excessive delight in earthly goods and pleasures.

Palestine. An ancient region of southwest Asia on the Mediterranean Sea comprising parts of present-day Israel, Jordan, and Egypt.

Persian. The language spoken by peoples of Iran and parts of Afghanistan and Pakistan.

Pillars of Islam, Five. The basis for the outward manifestation of the faith of *Islam:* that there is no deity except God and *Muhammad* is His *messenger,* the observance of prayer *(salat),* the payment of *zakat,* the pilgrimage *(hajj),* and the fast during *Ramadan (siyam).*

Polytheism. The belief in many gods.

Prophet, the. *Muhammad,* the *messenger* of God and last or "seal" of the *prophets* according to *Islam.*

Prophets. *Messengers* of God, the first of whom was *Adam* and the last *Muhammad* according to *Islam.* The *Qur'an* mentions twenty-five, most of whom are recognized in the Bible.

Psalms. A book of the *Torah* (Old Testament) consisting of songs of praise to God attributed to King *David.* In Arabic, "Zabur."

Qadaa. God's decree. See also *Qadar.*

Qadar. The belief that events take place according to the will of God. See also *Qadaa.*

Qibla. The direction toward the *Ka'aba* in *Mecca* from any place in the world.

Qiyam. A ritual prayer position in which the right hand is clasped lightly above the left wrist and held a little above the waist.

Quraish. The *Prophet's* tribe.

Qur'an (sometimes spelled "Koran"). The book of writings accepted by *Muslims* as revelations made to *Muhammad* by *Allah.*

Rakat. A unit or units of Islamic prayer.

Ramadan. Ninth month of the Islamic calendar, during which the faithful must observe a fast throughout daylight hours.

Rasul. "Messenger," one of the names given to each of the twenty-five *prophets* mentioned in the *Qur'an.*

Ruku. A ritual prayer position of bowing with the hands placed just above the knees.

Sa'i. During pilgrimage, the "hastening," or visit, to two hills in *Mecca* where *Hagar* and *Ishmael* found water and saved themselves from death.

Sadaqah. An act of charity; a voluntary contribution to the poor over and above *zakat*.

Sadaqat-ul-Fitr. See *Zakat-ul-Fitr*.

Salat. Prayer ritual observed by *Muslims* five times a day: at dawn, in the early afternoon, in the late afternoon, just after sunset, and at night.

Salatul Ibraheemiyah. A prayer honoring the *prophet Abraham*.

Sawn. See *Siyam*.

Seeyam. See *Siyam*.

Shaban. Eighth month of the Islamic calendar, on one day of which fasting is recommended.

Shahadah (also spelled "Tashahud"). The declaration of faith that there is no deity except God and *Muhammad* is His *messenger*. See also *Iman*.

Shari'ah. A complex code of law, grounded in divine revelation, which affects all aspects of life.

Shawwal. Tenth month of the Islamic calendar, during six days of which fasting is recommended.

Shirk. *Polytheism.*

Sidq. Truth—one of the four virtues ascribed to the *prophets* of *Islam*.

Sinai, Mount of. The place where *Moses* received the *Ten Commandments* from God, in the southern part of the Sinai Peninsula between ancient *Palestine* and Egypt.

Siyam (also spelled "Sawm" and "Seeyam"). Fasting; especially the fast during *Ramadan*.

Solomon's Temple. The Temple of Jerusalem erected under the direction of King Solomon in the tenth century B.C. and destroyed by the Babylonians in the sixth century B.C; site of *Islam's Farthest Mosque*.

Suhoor. The meal taken during the night at the time of the *Ramadan* fast.

Sujud. A ritual prayer position of prostration in which the forehead, nose, and fingers touch the floor.

Sunnah. The practice of the *Prophet;* additional, or nonobligatory, prayers in Muslim ritual.

Sura (also spelled "surah"). A chapter of the *Qur'an.*

Surah. See *Sura.*

Tabligh. Conveying the message of God completely—one of the four virtues ascribed to the *prophets* of *Islam.*

Takbir. A recitation of the prayer, "God is most Great."

Talbiya. Answer to God's call.

Taqwa. God-consciousness; an awareness of God and an acknowledgment of responsibility toward Him and toward fellow human beings.

Tarawih prayers. Optional prayers recited during *Ramadan* after the *'isha* (night) prayer.

Tashahud. See *Shahadah.*

Taurat. See *Torah.*

Tawaf. The ritual circumambulation of the *Ka'aba* during pilgrimage.

Tawheed. Faith in the unity of God.

Tayammum. Ritual dry cleaning of hands, face, and arms before prayer when one is unable to find water for *wudu.*

Thana. The song of praise to God.

Torah. Revelation given to *Moses;* the Old Testament. In Arabic, "Taurat."

Uhud, Battle of. A battle between the Meccans and the *Muslims* in 625, during which the *Prophet* was wounded but recovered.

Ulu'l-'Azm. A title of honor given to certain *prophets* distinguishing them as persons of determination and perseverance. The prophets so honored are *Muhammad, Noah* (Nuh), *Abraham* (Ibrahim), *Moses* (Musa), and *Jesus* ('Isa).

'Umra. The minor pilgrimage to *Mecca* as distinguished from *hajj,* the major pilgrimage.

Urdu. A literary language of Pakistan, also spoken in parts of India.

Wahy. Revelation from God.

Well of Zamzam. See *Zamzam, Well of.*

Wudu. Ritual washing before prayer of hands, mouth, nostrils, face, arms, head, and feet.

Yathrib. Another name for *Medina.*

Zabur. A Jewish woman who tried to poison *Muhammad* after the Battle of *Khaybar.*

Zakat. The fourth *Pillar of Islam*—a percentage of income collected once a year and distributed to the needy, travelers, students, orphans, widows, and the like. The literal meaning of the word is "purity."

Zakat-ul-Fitr (also spelled "Sadaqat-ul-Fitr"). Contribution given to the poor during *Ramadan.*

Zamzam, Well of. A spring in *Mecca* from which pilgrims drink during *hajj;* the place where *Hagar* and *Ishmael* found water and so saved themselves from death.

Zarathustra. A seventh- to sixth-century B.C. religious reformer and founder of Zoroastrianism, the religion of ancient Persia whose followers worshipped Ahura Mazda, the god of kindness and light.

Zuhr. The early afternoon prayer, consisting of four *rakat* said silently.